M000026100

# Reading Engagement
## Grade 3

By
JANET P. SITTER, Ph.D.

COPYRIGHT © 2005 Mark Twain Media, Inc.

ISBN 1-58037-287-2

Printing No. CD-404014

Mark Twain Media, Inc., Publishers
Distributed by Carson-Dellosa Publishing Company, Inc.

# Table of Contents

# Introduction

The goal of *Reading Engagement: Grade 3* is to help students improve their reading comprehension skills. The reading selections and reading guides in this book have been developed to provide instructional reading practice for below-average and/or reluctant readers, to provide independent reading activities for the average reader, and to provide supplemental reading for the more competent readers in your classroom.

By completing the readings and activities in *Reading Engagement: Grade 3,* your students will receive instruction, practice, and/or reinforcement in these strategies routinely practiced by good readers:

1. Good readers see reading as a comprehension process, not a decoding process.
2. Good readers relate what they are reading to what they already know.
3. Good readers decode rapidly, applying a number of word analysis skills to figure out unknown words.
4. Good readers know and recognize more words and have larger vocabularies.
5. Good readers monitor their comprehension and take action when they don't understand what they are reading.

*Reading Engagement: Grade 3* uses interesting text to focus students' motivation and interest on what they are reading. The activities in the Reading Guides help students make connections between what they are reading and what they already know. The vocabulary exercises help students not only build vocabulary but learn new words in meaningful ways. The

comprehension questions seek to improve the thinking skills of students by asking questions at the literal, interpretive, and applied levels of critical thinking. The Reading Guides provide support for comprehension before reading, during reading, and after reading. Students' comprehension is tested through a simple, informal reading assessment following each reading. And finally, each lesson contains one or more activities to extend students' understanding after reading.

Each lesson is designed for independent student use, though with reluctant or below-average readers, instruction may be necessary. Each lesson is independent of all of the other lessons and increases in difficulty as the student moves through them. Each lesson can be treated as a unit of instruction and can become part of the student's reading portfolio.

The more students read, the better readers they become. These readings are designed to help them become better readers.

# How To Use This Book

The reading lessons in this book are divided into four levels. Each level increases the difficulty of the reading, beginning with Level One, Lesson 1 at a 2.1 reading level and continuing with incremental jumps in reading difficulty, culminating in Level Four, Lesson 4 at a 4.0 reading level.

| Level One | Level Two | Level Three | Level Four |
|---|---|---|---|
| Lesson 1   2.1 | Lesson 1   2.7 | Lesson 1   3.0 | Lesson 1   3.6 |
| Lesson 2   2.3 | Lesson 2   2.8 | Lesson 2   3.3 | Lesson 2   3.7 |
| Lesson 3   2.4 | Lesson 3   2.9 | Lesson 3   3.4 | Lesson 3   3.8 |
| Lesson 4   2.5 | | | Lesson 4   4.0 |

Each lesson contains a short 100–600 word story with a Reading Guide. The instructional framework for the Reading Guides consists of activities to do before reading the selection, during the reading of the selection, and after reading the selection.

## BEFORE READING

The activities in the *Before Reading* section of the Reading Guides are intended to prepare the reader for the reading by:

a.   establishing a purpose for reading;

b.   building and activating background knowledge;

c.   connecting what is known to what is to be learned;

d.   presenting key concepts and vocabulary; and

e.   activating student interest and motivation.

## DURING READING

The activities in the *During Reading* section of the Reading Guides are intended to support the reader during the reading by:

a.   encouraging readers to read actively;

b.   guiding interactions between readers and text;

c.   using questions to activate critical thinking; and

d.   checking and expanding student comprehension skills.

# How To Use This Book (cont.)

## AFTER READING

The activities in the *After Reading* section of the guides are intended to assess and extend the reader's comprehension by:

a.  promoting thoughtful consideration of the text;
b.  supporting the reader's comprehension with Internet experiences;
c.  checking and evaluating the reader's comprehension; and
d.  extending the reader's understanding of the text.

Reading comprehension skills refer to a wide range of skills readers use to get meaning from text. While these skills develop over time, the lessons in *Reading Engagement: Grade 3* provide instruction, practice, and reinforcement in the following skills:

- Identifying details
- Stating main idea
- Inferring main idea
- Recalling details
- Inferring details
- Inferring cause and effect
- Following directions
- Determining sequence
- Locating reference
- Recalling information
- Summarizing ideas
- Identifying time sequence
- Retelling in own words
- Inferring author's purpose/intent

- Comparing and contrasting
- Drawing conclusions
- Making generalizations
- Recognizing structure and organization of text
- Predicting outcomes
- Evaluating text
- Judging author's qualifications
- Distinguishing facts from opinions
- Recognizing figurative language
- Identifying mood
- Understanding mental imagery
- Recognizing signal words
- Recognizing elements of the story

# Reading Level Analysis for Reading Selections

**Sample Begins: Dandy Dapper Dogs**
Sample Ends: The Dandy Dapper Dogs were a hit!
Words: 177
Difficult Words: 13
Sentences: 26
Syllables/Word: 1.34
Syllables/100 Words: 133.90
Monosyllabic Words/100 Words: 68.93
Polysyllabic Words/100 Words: 2.83
Sentences/100 Words: 14.69
Words/Sentence: 6.81
**Reading Grade Level: 2.1**

**Sample Begins: Manatees and Dugongs**
Sample Ends: dugongs will become extinct.
Words: 334
Difficult Words: 32
Sentences: 34
Syllables/Word: 1.36
Syllables/100 Words: 136.23
Monosyllabic Words/100 Words: 73.05
Polysyllabic Words/100 Words: 8.38
Sentences/100 Words: 13.77
Words/Sentence: 9.82
**Reading Grade Level: 2.3**

**Sample Begins: Sleepwalking**
Sample Ends: for elementary children.
Words: 282
Difficult Words: 29
Sentences: 36
Syllables/Word: 1.41
Syllables/100 Words: 141.32
Monosyllabic Words/100 Words: 71.18
Polysyllabic Words/100 Words: 11.11
Sentences/100 Words: 13.89
Words/Sentence: 7.83
**Reading Grade Level: 2.4**

**Sample Begins: The Cat's Pajamas**
Sample Ends: • Cats like to be cuddled.
Words: 234
Difficult Words: 24
Sentences: 28
Syllables/Word: 1.27
Syllables/100 Words: 126.50
Monosyllabic Words/100 Words: 81.20
Polysyllabic Words/100 Words: 6.41
Sentences/100 Words: 11.54
Words/Sentence: 8.36
**Reading Grade Level: 2.5**

**Sample Begins: Bring in the Clowns**
Sample Ends: and better about the world.
Words: 341
Difficult Words: 46
Sentences: 45
Syllables/Word: 1.39
Syllables/100 Words: 138.71
Monosyllabic Words/100 Words: 70.67
Polysyllabic Words/100 Words: 7.33
Sentences/100 Words: 13.20
Words/Sentence: 7.58
**Reading Grade Level: 2.7**

**Sample Begins: The Jewel of the Caribbean**
Sample Ends: a jewel in the Caribbean Sea.
Words: 182
Difficult Words: 29
Sentences: 27
Syllables/Word: 1.49
Syllables/100 Words: 148.90
Monosyllabic Words/100 Words: 65.93
Polysyllabic Words/100 Words: 14.84
Sentences/100 Words: 14.84
Words/Sentence: 6.74
**Reading Grade Level: 2.8**

**Sample Begins: Snowboarding**
Sample Ends: and water resistance.
Words: 246
Difficult Words: 63
Sentences: 22
Syllables/Word: 1.48
Syllables/100 Words: 148.16
Monosyllabic Words/100 Words: 67.42
Polysyllabic Words/100 Words: 12.75
Sentences/100 Words: 14.73
Words/Sentence: 11.18
**Reading Grade Level: 2.9**

**Sample Begins: Famous Firsts**
Sample Ends: Who is she?
Words: 541
Difficult Words: 71
Sentences: 58
Syllables/Word: 1.44
Syllables/100 Words: 143.61
Monosyllabic Words/100 Words: 69.57
Polysyllabic Words/100 Words: 10.66
Sentences/100 Words: 10.27
Words/Sentence: 9.33
**Reading Grade Level: 3.0**

**Sample Begins: When Is a Planet Not a Planet?**
Sample Ends: might not be a planet at all.
Words: 230
Difficult Words: 31
Sentences: 18
Syllables/Word: 1.44
Syllables/100 Words: 143.48
Monosyllabic Words/100 Words: 62.61
Polysyllabic Words/100 Words: 4.78
Sentences/100 Words: 7.83
Words/Sentence: 12.78
**Reading Grade Level: 3.3**

# Reading Level Analysis for Reading Selections

**Sample Begins: Hey, There, Buckaroo!**
Sample Ends: they are with their horses.
Words: 471
Difficult Words: 84
Sentences: 41
Syllables/Word: 1.45
Syllables/100 Words: 145.30
Monosyllabic Words/100 Words: 68.27
Polysyllabic Words/100 Words: 8.97
Sentences/100 Words: 9.85
Words/Sentence: 11.48
**Reading Grade Level: 3.4**

**Sample Begins: Did You Know …?**
Sample Ends: pigs during his lifetime?)
Words: 552
Difficult Words: 41
Sentences: 40
Syllables/Word: 1.49
Syllables/100 Words: 149.81
Monosyllabic Words/100 Words: 65.81
Polysyllabic Words/100 Words: 16.36
Sentences/100 Words: 8.90
Words/Sentence: 11.27
**Reading Grade Level: 3.6**

**Sample Begins: The Sun Queen**
Sample Ends: beautiful women of antiquity.
Words: 318
Difficult Words: 71
Sentences: 31
Syllables/Word: 1.62
Syllables/100 Words: 161.64
Monosyllabic Words/100 Words: 65.41
Polysyllabic Words/100 Words: 18.87
Sentences/100 Words: 10.38
Words/Sentence: 10.26
**Reading Grade Level: 3.7**

**Sample Begins: Travel Guide**
Sample Ends: and Clark Expedition a success.
Words: 356
Difficult Words: 79
Sentences: 30
Syllables/Word: 1.74
Syllables/100 Words: 173.60
Monosyllabic Words/100 Words: 58.43
Polysyllabic Words/100 Words: 20.23
Sentences/100 Words: 8.99
Words/Sentence: 11.87
**Reading Grade Level: 3.8**

**Sample Begins: Money Matters**
Sample Ends: piece of history in your hand!
Words: 390
Difficult Words: 81
Sentences: 26
Syllables/Word: 1.50
Syllables/100 Words: 149.49
Monosyllabic Words/100 Words: 70.51
Polysyllabic Words/100 Words: 11.80
Sentences/100 Words: 7.18
Words/Sentence: 15
**Reading Grade Level: 4.0**

Name: _____  Date: _____

# Level One: Lesson 1: Dandy Dapper Dogs

### Dandy Dapper Dogs

The children at the party sat down.
They were ready for the show.
They were happy to see the dogs.
The star of the show was Sybil.
Sybil did many tricks.
She liked balls and Frisbees.
Sybil answered the telephone.
The children laughed.

The children also liked Ramona.
Ramona jumped rope and climbed ladders.
She could also do tricks while rolling on a barrel.
Her best trick was opening the mailbox.
She got the mail and gave it to her trainer.
The children clapped and clapped for Ramona.

Tamako was the third dog to do tricks.
She watched Sybil's tricks.
She watched Ramona's tricks.
She was still learning how to be a "Dandy Dapper Dog."
Already she could flip for balls and Frisbees.
She could run a flyball course.
She is learning high jumping and chariot racing.

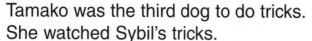

Sybil, Ramona, and Tamako were dressed in their party
costumes.
The children loved the dog show.
They laughed, cheered, and clapped for the trick dogs.
The Dandy Dapper Dogs were a hit!

Name: _____ Date: _____

 # Level One: Lesson 1: Dandy Dapper Dogs (cont.)

## Reading Guide for "Dandy Dapper Dogs"

Before reading, "Dandy Dapper Dogs," complete the **Before Reading** section of the Reading Guide.

## BEFORE READING

**A.   Prereading Activity:** Answer these questions about a pet.

1.   What kind of pet do you have at home?

_____

2.   If you don't have one, would you like to have one?

_____

3.   If you could have any pet you wanted, what would it be?

_____

4.   Is there anything special about your pet (real or imaginary)?

_____

5.   What is (or would be) your pet's name?

_____

Use the information above to write a three-sentence paragraph about your pet (real or imaginary).

_____

_____

_____

_____

_____

_____

_____

Share your paragraph with others.

Name: _____ Date: _____

# Level One: Lesson 1: Dandy Dapper Dogs (cont.)

## B. Vocabulary

1. Look at each drawing in Figure 1. Can you pronounce each dog's name?

**Sybil**
( sĭb′-əl )

**Ramona**
( rə - mō′ - nə )

**Tamako**
( tăm′-ə - kō )

**Figure 1: The "Stars"**

**trainer**
( trān′- ər )

**children**
( chĭl′- drən )

**Figure 2: The People**

2. What do the drawings in Figure 2 have to do with the drawings in Figure 1? (If you don't know, make a guess.)

_____

_____

_____

Name: _____  Date: _____

# Level One: Lesson 1: Dandy Dapper Dogs (cont.)

3. Look carefully at the drawings in Figure 3. On the line below each picture, write what you think the picture is.

_____   _____   _____

_____   _____   _____

**Figure 3: Tricky Things**

## C. Prereading Questions

1. What do you think this reading is going to be about?

_____

2. Read the questions in the **After Reading** section of this Reading Guide.

   a. Which question do you find the most interesting?

   _____

   _____

Name: _____ Date: _____

## Level One: Lesson 1: Dandy Dapper Dogs (cont.)

    b.   Which answer do you think will be hardest to find?

    _____

    _____

3.  What is your purpose for reading this story? Finish this sentence: I am reading to find out ...

_____

_____

## DURING READING

1.  Put a check mark in the margin next to the information that answers the questions in the **After Reading** section.

2.  Circle any words you don't know when you come to them in the passage.

3.  Put a question mark in the margin for anything you don't understand.

## AFTER READING

1.  READING THE LINES: Answer these questions by using information in the selection.

    a.   What is the main idea of this reading?

    _____

    _____

    b.   Where was the dog show?

    _____

    _____

Name: _____ Date: _____

 **Level One: Lesson 1: Dandy Dapper Dogs (cont.)**

c.  What was each dog's best trick?

1.  Sybil: _____

2.  Ramona: _____

3.  Tamako: _____

d.  Which sentence in the reading shows how much the children liked the dog show? Write it here.

_____

_____

_____

e.  Number these sentences in the order in which they happened in the story.

_____  Tamako flipped for balls and Frisbees.

_____  The children cheered.

_____  Sybil answered the telephone.

_____  Ramona got the mail from the mailbox.

_____  Ramona did tricks while rolling on a barrel.

2.  READING BETWEEN THE LINES: Answer these questions by inferring ideas in the selection.

a.  What would be a good topic sentence for this reading? Write one here.

_____

_____

_____

Name: _____ Date: _____

 **Level One: Lesson 1: Dandy Dapper Dogs (cont.)**

b.　Are Sybil, Ramona, and Tamako male or female dogs? How do you know?

_____

_____

_____

c.　Which dog do you think was the oldest? Youngest? Why?

_____

_____

_____

d.　What kind of dog would make a "Dandy Dapper Dog"?

_____

_____

_____

3.　READING BEYOND THE LINES: Answer these questions with your opinions.

a.　What kind of "party costumes" do you think the dogs were wearing?

_____

_____

b.　Which dog, do you think, did the best tricks? Why?

_____

_____

_____

c.　Would you like to see a trick-dog show like this? Why?

_____

_____

_____

Name: _____ Date: _____

# Level One: Lesson 1: Dandy Dapper Dogs (cont.)

**A.** Plan an animal show with the dogs and cats and other animals you and your friends have. Describe what tricks each animal will do. If you don't have a dog (or cat), then plan the perfect animal show (one with imaginary animals!). Write about it on the lines below.

_____

_____

_____

_____

_____

_____

_____

_____

**B.** Make a flyer on the computer that you might use to tell people about the dog show. Be sure to describe the show, introduce the stars of the show, and give the particulars: date, time, place, etc. Attach a copy of this flyer to the Reading Guide.

Name: _____ Date: _____

# Level One: Lesson 1: Dandy Dapper Dogs (cont.)

**C.** Research at the library or on the Internet how you might have your own Dandy Dapper Dog. Write down some of the ways you could train your dog. Then draw a picture of your dog doing a trick.

_____

_____

_____

_____

_____

_____

_____

_____

_____

Name: _____  Date: _____

# Level One: Lesson 2: Manatees and Dugongs

## Manatees and Dugongs

Manatees and dugongs are large, slow-moving sea mammals. They are very gentle. They live in warm, shallow, tropical waters. They spend their whole lives in the water. Because they are mammals, they must breathe air like you and me. They can hold their breath for about twenty minutes but usually come up for air every five minutes or so. They eat only plants. Manatees and dugongs can eat up to 100 pounds of plants in one day! This is probably more than you weigh. The mouths of manatees and dugongs are shaped differently from ours. Their lower lips and jaws have horny pads that help them grab plants. They have no front teeth, but their broad, flat, back teeth are good for grinding up plants. Manatees and dugongs can see, although they have very small eyes. They have no ears but can hear very well.

Manatees are about ten feet long and weigh about 1,000 pounds. Their babies are bigger and weigh more than most first graders. Their bodies are rounded, shaped like a seal's body. Usually they are light or dark gray in color. They have paddle-shaped flippers and flat, rounded tails. Manatees use their flippers like arms.

Dugongs have a two-pronged tail that they use for swimming. They also have front flippers like mana-tees. They use these flippers for balance and turning. They have a round head and a large snout. Like mana-tees, dugongs live in pairs or in groups of up to six animals.

**Manatee**

**Dugong**

Because these animals are so large, their only enemy is people. Every year, more people move near the warm coasts and rivers that are home to manatees and dugongs. Every year, there are fewer places for them to live and feed. People drive boats carelessly and too fast. They throw litter into the water. Some people chase or tease these gentle animals. Pollution kills the seagrass and other plants that they eat. If we don't stop this behavior, manatees and dugongs will become extinct.

Name: _____ Date: _____

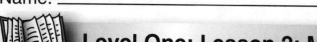

# Level One: Lesson 2: Manatees and Dugongs (cont.)

## Reading Guide for "Manatees and Dugongs"

### BEFORE READING

Before reading, "Manatees and Dugongs," complete the **Before Reading** section of the Reading Guide.

**A.  Prereading Activity**

Draw a picture of a manatee and a dugong. Don't worry if you don't know what they look like; use your imagination to draw what you think they might look like.

```



```

**B.  Prereading Questions**

1.  What do you think a manatee is?

    _____

    _____

    _____

2.  What do you think a dugong is?

    _____

    _____

    _____

Name: _____     Date: _____

# Level One: Lesson 2: Manatees and Dugongs (cont.)

3. Where might these creatures live?

_____

_____

4. What might these creatures eat?

_____

_____

When you finish, look at the picture of them on page 15.

## C. Vocabulary

Circle the correct definition for each of the following words:

1. tropical

   hard or rough          hot and humid          very wide

2. horny

   hard or rough          hot and humid          very wide

3. shallow

   mild or kind           wear away              not deep

4. mammal

   opponent               animal nose            warm-blooded

5. extinct

   opponent               to pester              died out

6. pollution

   animal nose            to draw in air         man-made waste

7. enemy

   opponent               to pester              died out

8. behavior

   to draw in air         to pester              person's or animal's actions

Name: _____ Date: _____

## Level One: Lesson 2: Manatees and Dugongs (cont.)

9. teases

   animal nose          pesters          not deep

10. snout

   animal nose          pesters          not deep

Choose three of the vocabulary words and use them together in one sentence. Use your imagination to create this sentence.

## D. Prereading Questions

1. What do you think this reading is going to be about?

   _____

   _____

2. Read the questions in the **After Reading** section of this Reading Guide so you will recognize the answers when you read them.

3. What is your purpose for reading? Finish this sentence: I am reading to find out ...

   _____

   _____

## DURING READING

1. Put a check mark in the margin next to the information that answers the questions in the **After Reading** section.

2. Circle any words you don't know when you come to them in the passage.

3. Put a question mark in the margin for anything you don't understand.

Name: _____ Date: _____

 **Level One: Lesson 2: Manatees and Dugongs (cont.)**

## AFTER READING

1. READING THE LINES: Answer these questions by using information in the selection.

   a. What is this story about?

   _____

   _____

   b. What are the differences between manatees and dugongs?

   _____

   _____

   _____

   c. How long can these sea creatures stay under water?

   _____

   _____

   d. Do manatees and dugongs have teeth? How do you know?

   _____

   _____

2. READING BETWEEN THE LINES: Answer these questions by inferring ideas in the selection.

   a. For what purpose do manatees use their flippers?

   _____

   _____

   b. Why are these animals on the endangered list?

   _____

   _____

Name: _____ Date: _____

## Level One: Lesson 2: Manatees and Dugongs (cont.)

    c.    What are three dangers that the manatees and dugongs face?

_____

_____

3.  READING BEYOND THE LINES: Answer these questions with your opinions.

    a.    What could be done about these dangers?

_____

_____

    b.    How do fast, careless boat drivers endanger these sea animals?

_____

_____

## ASSESSMENT/REINFORCEMENT

**A.**    Examine the drawings of the dugong and the mermaid. How are they the same? How are they different? Write your answers on your own paper.

**B.**    Some people believe that sailors saw manatees and thought they were mermaids, and this is how the mermaid legends started. Write a paragraph on your own paper about what you think about this belief.

Name: _____ Date: _____

 **Level One: Lesson 2: Manatees and Dugongs (cont.)**

**C.** Unscramble each word and use it to fill in the blanks for the sentences about manatees and dugongs. Write the circled letters at the bottom of the page to spell out the enemy of the manatees and dugongs.

1. Manatees and dugongs are large, slow-moving sea (LAMMASM).

   ___ ___ ___ ___ ___ ___ ___

2. They live in warm, shallow, (LCPROTIA) waters.

   ___ ___ ◯ ___ ___ ___ ___

3. Manatees and dugongs spend their whole lives in (TRWEA).

   ___ ___ ___ ◯ ___

4. They eat only plants, and can eat up to 100 (SNUOPD) in one day.

   ___ ◯ ___ ___ ___ ___

5. Manatees and dugongs have no front (TETHE). ___ ___ ___ ___ ___

6. Manatees are light or dark (GYAR) in color. ___ ___ ___ ___

7. Manatees use their (EPRFIPLS) like arms.

   ___ ___ ___ ___ ◯ ___ ___ ___

8. Dugongs have a two-pronged tail that they use for (MISWNIGM).

   ___ ___ ___ ___ ___ ___ ___ ___

9. Dugongs use their flippers for (CEBNAAL) and turning.

   ___ ___ ◯ ___ ___ ___ ___

10. If we aren't careful, manatees and dugongs will become (CTENXIT)

    ◯ ___ ___ ___ ___ ___ ___

** The only enemy of manatees and dugongs is: ◯ ◯ ◯ ◯ ◯ ◯

Name: _____ Date: _____

# Level One: Lesson 3: Sleepwalking

### Sleepwalking

Lots of kids walk in their sleep. One out of ten children is a sleepwalker. More boys sleepwalk than girls. Sleepwalking is common in children between six and twelve years old. Most sleepwalkers grow out of it as teenagers.

Sleepwalking is a sleep disorder. The sleepwalker partly wakes up during the night, but he or she is not fully awake. The child may walk around or do other things. A sleepwalker may sit up in bed. He may walk around the room. He may repeat certain actions. He may look dazed. His movements may be clumsy. A sleepwalker will not answer if you talk to him. Some sleepwalkers wander around the house. Usually the sleepwalker will walk right back to bed. He will go to sleep. He will not remember in the morning.

Scientists don't know exactly why kids sleepwalk. They think it happens to children who are in a deep, deep sleep. They think it might be because of stress. They think it might have something to do with maturation. They think kids with bad nightmares as preschoolers are more likely to sleepwalk. Scientists also don't know how to prevent it.

Another person may help the sleepwalker. He or she could gently lead the "walker" back to bed. He or she could keep the walker from dangerous accidents. He or she could keep the walker from going outside. But don't ever try to wake up a sleepwalker. Never yell at him or make loud noises. Never shake a sleepwalker.

Many children walk in their sleep. Some do funny or odd things. Many outgrow sleepwalking by middle school. Scientists do not think it is anything to worry about. They believe it is a common problem for elementary school children.

Name: _____ Date: _____

# Level One: Lesson 3: Sleepwalking (cont.)

## Reading Guide for "Sleepwalking"

### BEFORE READING

Before reading, "Sleepwalking," complete the **Before Reading** section of the Reading Guide.

### A.  Prereading Activity: Reading a Picture

Look at the drawings in Figure 1. What is going on? On the lines below, write down all of the things that you think are going on in these pictures.

**Figure 1**

_____

_____

_____

_____

_____

_____

_____

_____

Name: _____ Date: _____

# Level One: Lesson 3: Sleepwalking (cont.)

## B. Vocabulary: Synonyms

Synonyms are words that mean the same or nearly the same as other words. In each of the following sentences, fill in the blank after the bold word with a synonym from the Word Bank. The sentences are taken from the story.

| WORD BANK | | | | |
|---|---|---|---|---|
| kindly | disasters | sickness | awkward | discard |
| fret | bad dreams | growing up | roam | hazardous |

1. Sleepwalking is a sleep **disorder** _____.

2. His movements may be **clumsy** _____.

3. Some sleepwalkers **wander** _____ around the house.

4. They think it might have something to do with **maturation**

   _____.

5. They think kids with **nightmares** _____ as preschoolers are more likely to sleepwalk.

6. He or she could **gently** _____ lead the "walker" back to bed.

7/8. He or she could keep the walker from **dangerous** _____

   **accidents** _____.

9. Many **outgrow** _____ sleepwalking by middle school.

10. Scientists do not think it is something to **worry** _____ about.

Name: _____ Date: _____

# Level One: Lesson 3: Sleepwalking (cont.)

## C. Prereading Questions

1. What do you think this reading is going to be about?

   _____

   _____

   _____

2. Read the questions in the **After Reading** section of this Reading Guide.

   a. Which question do you find the most interesting?

   _____

   _____

   b. Which answer do you think will be hardest to find?

   _____

   _____

3. What is your purpose for reading this story? Finish this sentence: I am reading to find out ...

   _____

   _____

## DURING READING

1. Put a check mark in the margin next to the information that answers the questions in the **After Reading** section.

2. Circle any words you don't know when you come to them in the passage.

3. Put a question mark in the margin for anything you don't understand.

25

Name: _____ Date: _____

# Level One: Lesson 3: Sleepwalking (cont.)

## AFTER READING

1. READING THE LINES: Answer these questions by using information in the selection.

   a. What are the ages of children who sleepwalk?

   _____

   _____

   b. What kind of disorder is sleepwalking?

   _____

   _____

   c. What are some things kids do when they sleepwalk?

   _____

   _____

   d. If you see a kid sleepwalking, what should you NOT do?

   _____

   _____

   e. What does the word *dazed* mean in line 7?

   _____

   _____

2. READING BETWEEN THE LINES: Answer these questions by inferring ideas in the selection.

   a. What characteristics do sleepwalkers have?

   _____

   _____

   _____

Name: _____ Date: _____

# Level One: Lesson 3: Sleepwalking (cont.)

b.  What does the word *common* mean in line 2?

_____

_____

c.  Is sleepwalking a serious problem for elementary school children? Why
    or why not?

_____

_____

3.  READING BEYOND THE LINES: Answer these questions with your opin-
    ions.
    a.  Why do more boys sleepwalk than girls? State your opinion and the
        reason(s) why you think as you do.

_____

_____

_____

_____

    b.  The author says never to shake or wake a sleepwalker but doesn't say
        why. What do you think the reason is?

_____

_____

_____

_____

    c.  Do you know anyone who sleepwalks? Are you a sleepwalker?

_____

_____

_____

27

Name: _____ Date: _____

 # Level One: Lesson 3: Sleepwalking (cont.)

## ASSESSMENT/REINFORCEMENT

**A.** If you want more information on sleepwalking, you could check out these websites:

        www.allkids.org/Epstein/Articles/Sleepwalking.html
        www.health.yahoo.com/centers/parenting.htm
        www.stanford.edu/~dement/slpwalking.htm

**B.** Find someone that you know or someone in your family who has sleepwalked. Interview them about an interesting sleepwalking experience. Write about the experience in story form.

_____

_____

_____

_____

_____

_____

_____

_____

_____

_____

_____

_____

_____

Name: _____ Date: _____

# Level One: Lesson 3: Sleepwalking (cont.)

## C.  Sleepwalking Crossword Puzzle

**Directions:** Complete each of the sentences from the reading and fill in the crossword puzzle. Look at the reading selection if you need help.

**ACROSS**

4.  Lots of kids _____ in their sleep.
5.  No one should ever _____ a sleepwalker.
6.  Most sleepwalkers grow out of it as _____.
10. A sleepwalker may _____ certain actions.
11. A sleepwalker may look dazed, or his movements may be _____.
12. Causes for sleepwalking could be _____ or maturation.
14. Someone can help the sleepwalker by keeping him from _____ accidents.
16. A sleepwalker won't usually _____ his actions.
19. You should never _____ a sleepwalker.

**DOWN**

1.  _____ don't know exactly why kids sleepwalk.
2.  One out of ten children is a _____.
3.  Scientists don't know how to _____ sleepwalking.
5.  Scientists don't think sleepwalking is anything to _____ about.
7.  The sleepwalker is not fully _____.
8.  Sleepwalking is a sleep _____.
9.  It's possible that kids sleepwalk because they are in a deep, deep _____.
13. When sleepwalking, the sleepwalker will not _____ if you talk to him.
15. Many children _____ sleepwalking by middle school.
17. More _____ sleepwalk than girls.
18. _____, the sleepwalker will walk right back to bed.

Name: _____ Date: _____

# Level One: Lesson 4: "The Cat's Pajamas"

### "The Cat's Pajamas"

"The cat's pajamas" is an old saying, like "Cat got your tongue?" and "It's raining cats and dogs." Cats are the most popular pets in the United States. Here are some interesting facts about cats that maybe you didn't know:

- Popular cat names are Max, Sassy, Sam, Simba, and Princess.
- Cats have very good hearing.
- Cats have four toes on their back paws and five toes on their front paws.
- Cats like people, but they worry most about territorial issues.
- Cats lick people to show that they like them.
- Cats live 14–20 years, and some cats can live as long as 30 years.
- Cats (and dogs) cannot see color.
- Aspirin is poisonous to cats.
- Cats can get AIDS and cancer.
- Cats' eyes reflect light, but they do not glow in the dark. A cat's night vision is six times better than a human's.
- Cats are primarily nocturnal animals.
- A cat cannot see directly under its nose. This is why cats cannot find food bits on the floor.
- Cats are carnivores.
- Most cats have no eyelashes.
- Many cats do not like milk; milk may even make them sick.
- White cats can get sunburned.
- You can tell a cat's mood by looking into its eyes. A frightened or excited cat has large, round pupils. An angry cat has narrow pupils.
- There are more than 100 different breeds of cat.
- Cats sleep 16–18 hours a day.
- Cats like to be cuddled.

Name: _____ Date: _____

 # Level One: Lesson 4: "The Cat's Pajamas" (cont.)

## Reading Guide for "The Cat's Pajamas"

Before reading, "The Cat's Pajamas," complete the **Before Reading** section of the Reading Guide.

## BEFORE READING

**A.** Write at least three sentences about your pet or pets. If you don't have a pet, write about the one you would like to have.

_____

_____

_____

_____

_____

_____

_____

_____

**B.** Discuss these questions with your classmates.

1. How many people wrote about Cats? Dogs? Other pets?

2. What was the most popular kind of pet? Why do you think that is?

**C. KWL Chart**

1. What do you know about cats? Fill in the cat in Figure 1 on page 32 with all of the information you know about cats.

2. What would you like to know about cats? Fill in the Persian Cat in Figure 2 on page 32 with all of the questions you have about cats.

31

Name: _____  Date: _____

# Level One: Lesson 4: "The Cat's Pajamas" (cont.)

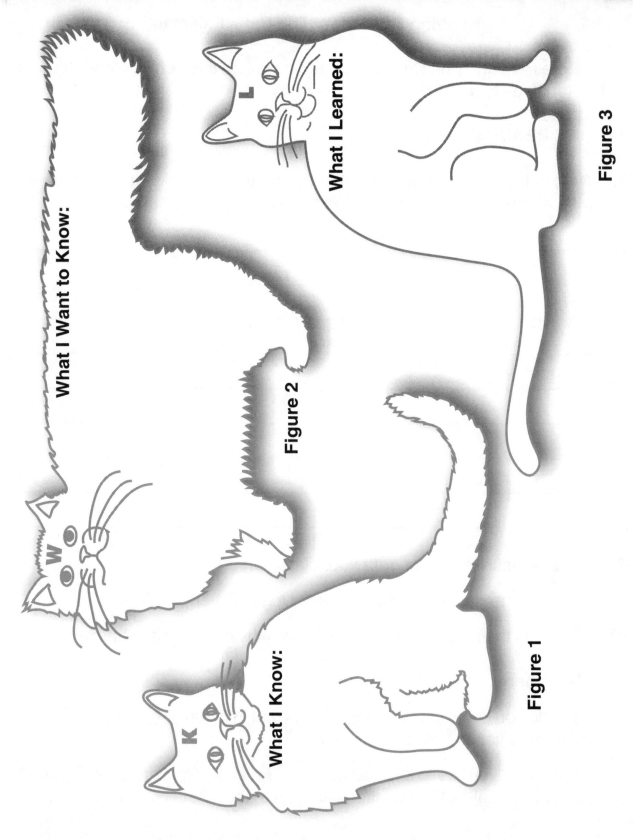

**What I Learned:**

**L**

Figure 3

**What I Want to Know:**

**W**

Figure 2

**What I Know:**

**K**

Figure 1

Name: _____ Date: _____

## Level One: Lesson 4: "The Cat's Pajamas" (cont.)

As you prepare to read the selection, complete the activities in the **During Reading** section.

### DURING READING

### A. Vocabulary

The following words may (or may not) give you some difficulty when reading.

| | | | |
|---|---|---|---|
| __ popular | __ territorial | __ aspirin | __ poisonous |
| __ reflect | __ vision | __ eyelashes | __ sunburned |
| __ frightened | __ excited | __ angry | __ breed |
| __ cuddled | __ carnivores | __ nocturnal | |

Decide if the word (as used in the reading selection) is an adjective (describes something), a noun (person, place, thing), or a verb (action word). Put an "A" in front of the adjectives, an "N" in front of the nouns, and a "V" in front of the verbs. Compare with a friend.

### B. Reading

1. Read the title of the selection. What do you think it means?

   _____

   _____

2. What do you think this selection is about?

   _____

   _____

3. Finish this sentence, "I am reading to find out ..."

   _____

   _____

4. Read the selection, "The Cat's Pajamas."

Name: _____ Date: _____

 **Level One: Lesson 4: "The Cat's Pajamas" (cont.)**

When you finish reading the selection, complete the **After Reading** section of the Reading Guide.

## AFTER READING

1. READING THE LINES: Answer these questions by using information in the selection.

   a. What are some popular names for cats?

   _____

   _____

   b. Why do cats lick people?

   _____

   _____

   c. How do you tell what mood your cat is in?

   _____

   _____

2. READING BETWEEN THE LINES: Answer these questions by inferring ideas in the selection.

   a. What does the word *territorial* mean in the phrase "worry most about territorial issues"?

   _____

   _____

   b. Why shouldn't you give milk to a cat?

   _____

   _____

Name: _____ Date: _____

# Level One: Lesson 4: "The Cat's Pajamas" (cont.)

c. How would you make friends with a cat?

_____

_____

d. Compare a cat to a dog. Which makes a better pet?

_____

_____

e. Is the author of this selection a cat lover? How can you tell?

_____

_____

3. READING BEYOND THE LINES: Answer these questions with your opinions.

a. How could you keep a white cat from getting sunburned?

_____

_____

b. What is the relationship between cats and humans?

_____

_____

c. If you got a new kitten, what are some ways you could make sure your kitten liked her people?

_____

_____

Name: _____ Date: _____

# Level One: Lesson 4: "The Cat's Pajamas" (cont.)

d.  Do you think you could train a cat to use a toilet?

_____

_____

4.  Now that you have learned about cats, go back to the KWL Chart/Cat Worksheet on page 32 and fill in the lines on Figure 3: Burmese Cat with what you have learned.

## ASSESSMENT/REINFORCEMENT

## A.  The Cat's Pajamas: True/False

**Directions:** Answer each of the questions "T" for true or "F" for false, based on what you read and have learned about cats.

_____ 1.  Cats do not like to be held and cuddled.

_____ 2.  Cats are good at seeing and hearing but not so good at smelling.

_____ 3.  Cats have more toes on their front paws than on their back paws.

_____ 4.  Cats do not suffer from loneliness like dogs and humans do.

_____ 5.  Cats will kill and eat small animals like birds, fish, snakes, etc.

_____ 6.  Cats are more active at night than they are during the day.

_____ 7.  Cats do not have very good night vision.

_____ 8.  You can tell a cat's mood by looking at its body language.

_____ 9.  Cats live longer than people.

_____ 10.  If your cat is sick, you should give it an aspirin.

Name: _____ Date: _____

 # Level One: Lesson 4: "The Cat's Pajamas" (cont.)

## B.　The Cat's Pajamas: Homophone Activity

**Directions:** Homophones are words that sound the same but are spelled differently and have different meanings. Circle the correct homophone(s) to complete each sentence.

1. Cats can ( here, hear ) ( very, vary ) well.

2. White cats should ( knot, not ) stay ( inn, in ) the ( sun, son ) (to, too, two ) long.

3. Cats and dogs can't ( sea, see ) color.

4. Cats can ( sea, see ) much better at ( knight, night ) than humans.

5. You can tell a cat's mood ( buy, by ) looking into ( its, it's ) eyes.

6. Cats sleep 16–18 ( hours, ours ) a day.

7. Cats like ( two, too, to ) ( bee, be ) cuddled.

8. You should ( not, knot ) give aspirin to cats.

9. Did you ( know, no ) that ( they're, there, their ) are over 100 different breeds of cat?

10. Cats have ( for, four ) toes on ( their, there, they're ) back ( pause, paws ).

11. ( Sum, Some ) cats live as long as 30 years.

12. Most cats have ( no, know ) eyelashes.

13. If cats are carnivores, does that mean they eat ( meet, meat ) ( ore, or ) plants?

14. A cat cannot ( see, sea ) directly under ( its, it's ) ( knows, nose ).

15. If you give milk ( two, too, to ) ( you're, your ) cat, it may get sick.

Name: _____ Date: _____

# Level Two: Lesson 4: Bring in the Clowns

### Bring in the Clowns

What is a clown? How do you become a clown? Where do clowns work? What does it take to be a clown? You will be able to answer these questions after reading this story.

A clown is a performer. A clown plays the fool. He or she plays practical jokes on people. A clown does tricks. A clown makes people laugh.

There are several ways to learn how to be a clown. One of the best ways is to go to college. Clown College offers classes in acrobatics and acting. New clowns study balloon twisting, face painting, and magic tricks. There are other ways to learn how to be a clown. You could learn from another clown or on your own.

To be a clown takes a special kind of person. Good clowns love performing. They enjoy making people laugh. They are creative and confident. A good clown has good hand-eye coordination. This helps in juggling and balancing. Clowns enjoy working with children.

Clowns work in circuses. They also per-form at children's parties. They are on televi-sion shows. Clowns work as buskers and at fairs. Clowns work in rodeos. Clowns can also work as teachers in clown schools and camps. Clowns can work in the movies. They are ac-tors, stunt doubles, and comedians.

There are many famous clowns. Bozo the Clown had his own television show. Mil-lions of people recognized Bozo by his red hair, clown suit, and clown makeup. Maybe more than a billion people recognize Ronald McDonald. Ronald is so famous that he has his own website at http://www.ronald.com/. Another famous clown is Clarabell. Clarabell Hornblower was a clown on a television show called *The Howdy Doody Show*. She never spoke. When she wanted to say some-thing, she blew the twin bicycle horns on a box around her waist. She also carried a bottle of seltzer water in that box. Anyone she didn't like she sprayed with water.

A good clown entertains others. A clown's work is to make people feel better about themselves and better about the world.

Name: _____ Date: _____

 # Level Two: Lesson 4: Bring in the Clowns (cont.)

### Reading Guide for "Bring in the Clowns"

## BEFORE READING

Before reading, "Bring in the Clowns," complete the **Before Reading** section of the Reading Guide.

## A. Prereading Activity: What Do You Know?

1. What do you know about clowns? Make a list of everything you know or think you know about clowns.

_____

_____

_____

_____

## B. Vocabulary: Clown Words

**Directions:** Place the words in the correct boxes below.

performing    famous    comedian    movies
circus    juggling    television    balancing
acrobatics    coordinated    balloon twisting    confident
rodeos    creative    parties

| A<br>Words that describe<br>a clown | B<br>Words that show<br>what a clown can do | C<br>Words that show<br>where a clown might work |
|---|---|---|
| _____ | _____ | _____ |
| _____ | _____ | _____ |
| _____ | _____ | _____ |
| _____ | _____ | _____ |

Name: _____ Date: _____

 **Level Two: Lesson 4: Bring in the Clowns (cont.)**

## C.  Homophone Activity

**Directions:** Homophones are words that sound the same but are spelled differently and have different meanings. Circle the correct homophone(s) to complete each sentence.

1.  ( Due, Do, Dew ) ( ewe, you ) ( know, no ) how ( too, two, to ) become a clown?

2.  ( Their, There, They're ) are many ( ways, weighs ) ( to, too, two ) become a clown.

3.  Going ( to, too, two ) Clown College is ( won, one ) of the best (weighs, ways ) to become a clown.

4.  It takes a special kind of person ( two, too, to ) ( bee, be ) a clown.

5.  Clowns work ( in, inn ) circuses and at ( fares, fairs ).

6.  (They're, There, Their ) are many famous clowns — ( too, two, to ) of them are Ronald McDonald and Clarabell Hornblower.

7.  Ronald McDonald is ( sow, so, sew ) famous that he has his own website.

8.  On *The Howdy Doody Show*, Clarabell Hornblower didn't speak; instead, she ( blue, blew ) bicycle horns when she wanted ( too, two, to ) say something.

9.  ( Eye, I ) think ( its, it's ) funny when a clown's (flour, flower ) squirts another clown in the ( eye, I ).

10. ( I, eye ) think ( ewe, you ) ( wood, would ) make a ( grate, great ) clown!

Name: _____ Date: _____

# Level Two: Lesson 4: Bring in the Clowns (cont.)

## D. Prereading Questions

1. What do you think this reading is going to be about?

   _____

   _____

   _____

2. Read the questions in the **After Reading** section of this Reading Guide.

   a.  Which question do you find the most interesting?

   _____

   _____

   b.  Which answer do you think will be hardest to find?

   _____

   _____

3. What is your purpose for reading this story? Finish this sentence: I am reading to find out ...

   _____

   _____

## DURING READING

1. Put a check mark in the margin next to the information that answers the questions in the **After Reading** section.

2. Circle any words you don't know when you come to them in the passage.

3. Put a question mark in the margin for anything you don't understand.

Name: _____ Date: _____

 **Level Two: Lesson 4: Bring in the Clowns (cont.)**

## AFTER READING

1. **READING THE LINES:** Answer these questions by using information in the selection.

   a.  What is a clown?

   _____

   _____

   _____

   b.  Make a list of the ways a person could learn to be a clown.

   _____

   _____

   _____

   c.  Where does a clown work?

   _____

   _____

   d.  Why does a clown need good hand-eye coordination?

   _____

   _____

   e.  Name a famous clown.

   _____

2. **READING BETWEEN THE LINES:** Answer these questions by inferring ideas in the selection.

   a.  What does the sentence, "A clown plays the fool" mean?

   _____

   _____

   _____

## Level Two: Lesson 4: Bring in the Clowns (cont.)

b. Why does it take a special type of person to be a clown?

_____

_____

c. What is a practical joke?

_____

_____

d. What does a clown who works in a rodeo do?

_____

_____

3. READING BEYOND THE LINES: Answer these questions with your opinions.

a. Some children are afraid of clowns. Why do you think they are afraid?

_____

_____

_____

b. Would you make a good clown? Why or why not?

_____

_____

_____

c. Who, in your opinion, is more famous, Bozo the Clown or Ronald McDonald? Why?

_____

_____

_____

Name: _____ Date: _____

## Level Two: Lesson 4: Bring in the Clowns (cont.)

### ASSESSMENT/REINFORCEMENT

**A.** What type of clown would you like to be? What would your makeup and costume look like? After thinking about it, draw a picture of yourself in makeup and costume.

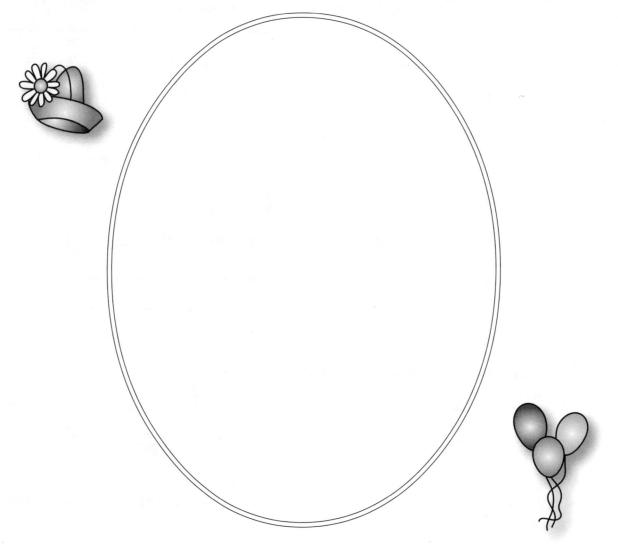

**B.** Clowns are good at making faces. Are you? Practice making faces in front of a mirror.

**C.** If you would like to learn more about clowns, check out these websites:

www.clownsofamerica.org　　　www.theclownmuseum.org

Name: _____ Date: _____

# Level Two: Lesson 4: Bring in the Clowns (cont.)

## D. Bring in the Clowns: Word Search

**Directions:** Find and circle the clown words from the word bank in the word search below. Words may be printed forward, backward, up, down, or diagonally.

```
G U T U O R O N A L D M C D O N A L D Y H I J R
H B Z X R A S T U N T D O U B L E S I E J R U Y
O O I O A C T W V I H G X P D D U R V U N U I F
V Z M E C Z K S N O O L L A B Y E R S Q P T R F
F O C N L Z C R D O M A G I C T R I C K S S W M
Q T L H O G E Q C J N Z C W Y D A L U R M N G M
Q H A C W S P Q O C M O A N A D N F C E K N N A
E E R D N R R Q R W L C I K K N K F J K L R I D
Y C A W S I A O L P B O N S A C T O R S E T N V
N L B G U A S C W L B D W E I Z E K E L Q B I R
L O E E I F A L R U K T S N U V V O N Q G E A K
Y W L W T L C J L O B S E J C Y E K I I A S T U
N N L M D B C D N P B O Q I Z O Z L G T W F R J
G Q F K B C O T Z E F A G M T J L N E F E A E Q
H H L Z V C U G W R I P T U E K N L E T Y C T D
J I S V H S L N P F Q U T I J L H O E N E E N M
M M R O G R M I A O C E L P C B U B E G Z P E L
D A E T S O D C O R C K N A O S J Q L Q E A X R
R S K W G S X N N M K A S J U Z G L G L G I N D
W U S P X O Q A K I M M U N Q G S U G L F N V P
G X U G B E I L H N D Y C C Y T H F U D F T B B
V P B K U D H A Q G D B L W M M I Y J A U D L S
R E I F V O Z B E V H L H D K L T H O F E C R V
U P U K U R E J F E D S U C R I C C X A T D O C
```

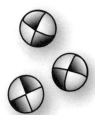

## Word Bank

| | | | |
|---|---|---|---|
| acrobatics | actors | balancing | balloons |
| Bozo the Clown | buskers | circus | Clarabell |
| Clown College | clown suit | entertaining | face paint |
| fairs | juggle | laugh | magic tricks |
| makeup | performing | rodeos | Ronald McDonald |
| stunt doubles | television | | |

Name: _____  Date: _____

# Level Two: Lesson 2: The Jewel of the Caribbean

## The Jewel of the Caribbean

Jamaica is an island. It is very beautiful. It has mountains, rivers, forests, beaches, caves, and waterfalls. Jamaica means "Land of Wood and Water."

Jamaica is surrounded by a sea full of beautiful fish. The shallow water makes it easy to see them. The stingrays get so close you can pet them.

The beaches of Jamaica sparkle. The sand is white. The water is blue. The coconut trees are tall.

The Fern Gully rain forest is lush. More than 3,000 flowering plants grow in the rain forest. The forest hides majestic waterfalls. The famous Dunns River Falls are hidden in the forest. Water splashes down more than 600 feet. The Falls are awesome. Fern Gully is stunning.

The weather of Jamaica is perfect. It is warm and sunny all year. The rain that falls keeps the rain forest hot and humid. This is good for the flowering plants. The weather makes the Jamaican beaches very inviting.

Jamaica has brilliant sunsets. The sun setting over the ocean paints the sky a breathtaking red. Jamaica is a jewel in the Caribbean Sea.

Name: _____ Date: _____

# Level Two: Lesson 2: The Jewel of the Caribbean (cont.)

## Reading Guide for "The Jewel of the Caribbean"

### BEFORE READING

Before reading, "The Jewel of the Caribbean," complete the **Before Reading** section of the Reading Guide.

### A.  Prereading Activity: Jamaica

"Read" the picture in Figure 1. Then see how many different things you can find in the picture, and write them on your own paper.

**Figure 1**

47

Name: _____ Date: _____

 **Level Two: Lesson 2: The Jewel of the Caribbean (cont.)**

## B. Vocabulary

1. Match the adjective with the noun as it is used in the reading selection.

| WORD BANK |
| --- |
| beautiful |
| perfect |
| flowering |
| brilliant |
| majestic |
| coconut |
| shallow |
| inviting |
| lush |
| white |

a. _____ water

b. _____ fish

c. _____ trees

d. _____ plants

e. _____ rain forest

f. _____ sunsets

g. _____ waterfalls

h. _____ beaches

i. _____ weather

j. _____ sand

2. Here are some more words from "The Jewel of the Caribbean." The pronunciation is given. You must spell the word.

a. jōō′ əl                                  _____

b. stĭng′rā                                _____

c. sə round′ ĕd                         _____

d. jə mā′ kə                             _____

e. kār′ə bē′ ən  or  kə rĭb′ ē ən    _____

Name: _____ Date: _____

## Level Two: Lesson 2: The Jewel of the Caribbean (cont.)

### C. Prereading Questions

1. What do you think this reading is going to be about?

   _____

   _____

2. Read the questions in the **After Reading** section of this Reading Guide.

   a. Which question do you find the most interesting?

   _____

   _____

   b. Which answer do you think will be hardest to find?

   _____

   _____

3. What is your purpose for reading this story? Finish this sentence: I am reading to find out ...

   _____

   _____

### DURING READING

1. Put a check mark in the margin next to the information that answers the questions in the **After Reading** section.

2. Circle any words you don't know when you come to them in the passage.

3. Put a question mark in the margin for anything you don't understand.

Name: _____ Date: _____

 **Level Two: Lesson 2: The Jewel of the Caribbean (cont.)**

## AFTER READING

1. READING THE LINES: Answer these questions by using information in the selection.

   a.  What does the word *Jamaica* mean?

   _____

   _____

   b.  Jamaica is completely surrounded by what body of water?

   _____

   _____

   c.  What are the beaches of Jamaica like?

   _____

   _____

   d.  What are some things you might see in the rain forest?

   _____

   _____

   e.  What does "breathtaking" mean?

   _____

   _____

2. READING BETWEEN THE LINES: Answer these questions by inferring ideas in the selection.

   a.  What is a stingray?

   _____

   _____

Name: _____ Date: _____

## Level Two: Lesson 2: The Jewel of the Caribbean (cont.)

b.   Why does the author consider Jamaica "the jewel of the Caribbean"?

_____

_____

3.   READING BEYOND THE LINES: Answer these questions with your opinions.

a.   Of the following, who would be most likely to write this story? Why?

1.   an island native
2.   a tourist
3.   a travel agent
4.   a banker

b.   Have you ever visited Jamaica? Would you like to go to Jamaica? Why?

_____

_____

_____

c.   What do you think the natives of Jamaica are like? Why?

_____

_____

_____

## ASSESSMENT/REINFORCEMENT

A.   Plan a Jamaican day. Research the island and its people. Copy native dress and cultural activities, especially the food.

B.   Watch the movie, *Pirates of the Caribbean*. Watch for scenes of the island. Did the moviemaker shoot scenes on the island of Jamaica? Why do you think so?

_____

_____

Name: _____ Date: _____

## Level Two: Lesson 2: The Jewel of the Caribbean (cont.)

### C. Word Scramble

**Directions:** Using the reading, "The Jewel of the Caribbean," unscramble the words describing some of the features of Jamaica.

1. UCTNOOC ETSER _____
2. NLSPTA _____
3. SBCHEEA _____
4. IWETH ADNS _____
5. LERWSATLAF _____
6. TNUSSES _____
7. NARI EOFRTS _____
8. LBUTAFEIU SIFH _____
9. UYSNN EERWHAT _____
10. UBEL RWETA _____

**D.** Imagine that you are visiting the island of Jamaica. Draw what you see.

Name: _____ Date: _____

# Level Two: Lesson 3: Snowboarding

## Snowboarding

### READ

Snowboarding is like surfing on snow. Snowboarders use a wide ski like a skateboard. It is ridden in a surfing position down a snow-covered hill. Tom Sims built the first snowboard in 1963. He modified his skateboard so it would slide on snow. Two other guys were working on the same idea. Jake Carpenter used what he knew about skiing to improve snowboarding. Dimitrije Melovich, an experienced surfer, based his snowboard designs on surfboard designs.

### STOP

1. Who invented snowboarding?

   _____

   _____

2. What three sports contributed to the sport of snowboarding?

   _____

   _____

3. To what does the word *It* in the third sentence refer?

   _____

   _____

Name: _____ Date: _____

# Level Two: Lesson 3: Snowboarding (cont.)

## READ

Snowboarding is the sport of sliding downhill over snow on a snowboard. This is a rather easy sport to learn. Snowboarders ride a wide board in a surfing position. Olympic snowboarding began in the 1998 Winter Games. There were two events for the competition: the giant slalom and the halfpipe. The giant slalom is skiing (or snowboarding) downhill by passing through a number of gates. In the halfpipe, riders use a large, snow-covered trench to launch themselves into the air where they perform various acrobatic tricks.

## STOP

4. Do you think snowboarding is more like skiing, surfing, or skateboarding? Why?

   _____

   _____

   _____

5. When did snowboarding become an Olympic event?

   _____

6. Halfpipe is where snowboarders show their individual skills. What is the best trick you've ever seen in snowboarding?

   _____

   _____

   _____

7. Would you like to snowboard? Why or why not?

   _____

   _____

   _____

Name: _____ Date: _____

## Level Two: Lesson 3: Snowboarding (cont.)

8. What does the word *launch* mean in the last sentence?

_____

_____

_____

**READ**

    To snowboard, a person needs a board, bindings, and boots. Clothing suitable to the weather is also necessary. Boards come in different lengths, depending on the size of the rider and the type of riding the person does. The bindings are used to hold the boots to the board. Layering is the best way to dress for snowboarding. It is important to have an inside layer for warmth, a middle layer for insulation, and an outer layer for wind and water resistance.

**STOP**

9. What equipment does a snowboarder need?

_____

_____

10. Why is it important for a snowboarder to dress for the weather?

_____

_____

_____

_____

_____

_____

55

Name: _____ Date: _____

# Level Two: Lesson 3: Snowboarding (cont.)

## Reading Guide for "Snowboarding"

### BEFORE READING

Before reading, "Snowboarding," complete the **Before Reading** section of the Reading Guide.

### A.  Prereading Activity

| A | B | C | D |

1.  Identify the sport being performed in each of the drawings.

   a.   A is _____

        B is _____

        C is _____

        D is _____

   b.   How are these drawings alike?

   _____

   _____

   _____

   c.   How are they different?

   _____

   _____

   _____

Name: _____ Date: _____

 **Level Two: Lesson 3: Snowboarding (cont.)**

## B. Vocabulary

**Directions:** These words are in the reading. First say the words aloud to yourself. Then write them in alphabetical order on the lines below.

technology　　　　giant slalom　　　　launch
Olympics　　　　　halfpipe　　　　　　acrobatic
competition　　　　trench　　　　　　　bindings
experienced　　　　surfing　　　　　　　resistance

_____

_____

_____

_____

## C. Prereading Questions

1. What do you think this reading is going to be about?

_____

_____

2. Read the questions in the **After Reading** section of this Reading Guide.

   a. Which question do you find the most interesting?

   _____

   _____

   b. Which answer do you think will be hardest to find?

   _____

   _____

3. What is your purpose for reading this story? Finish this sentence: I am reading to find out ...

_____

_____

Name: _____ Date: _____

# Level Two: Lesson 3: Snowboarding (cont.)

## DURING READING

1. Put a check mark in the margin next to the information that answers the questions in the **After Reading** section.

2. Circle any words you don't know when you come to them in the passage.

3. Put a question mark in the margin for anything you don't understand.

4. Answer the questions in the reading selection as you read each section.

## AFTER READING

1. READING THE LINES: Answer these questions by using information in the selection.

a. What do you know now about snowboarding that you didn't know before?

_____

_____

_____

b. Without looking, what two vocabulary words do you now know?

_____

_____

c. Would you like to learn more about snowboarding? Why or why not?

_____

_____

_____

## ASSESSMENT/REINFORCEMENT

**A.** What is the difference between a snowboard, a skateboard, and a surfboard? Do some research, and then draw the three, highlighting the differences.

**B.** If you haven't snowboarded yourself, then find someone who has. Ask him or her to describe the experience. Write the story on your own paper and include many adjectives.

Name: _____ Date: _____

## Level Two: Lesson 3: Snowboarding (cont.)

### C.  Snowboarding: Fill-in-the-Blank Activity

**Directions:** Read each sentence, and then write the word in the blank to the right of that sentence. The first letter has been given to you.

1.  Snowboarding is like _____ on snow.  **S** _____

2.  Clothing suitable to the weather is _____ for snowboarding.  **N** _____

3.  Wear an _____ layer of clothing for wind and water resistance.  **O** _____

4.  Layering clothing is essential for _____ when snowboarding.  **W** _____

5.  _____ are used to hold the boots to the board.  **B** _____

6.  Snowboarding became an _____ event in the 1998 Winter Games.  **O** _____

7.  In the halfpipe, snowboarders perform _____ tricks.  **A** _____

8.  A snowboard is _____ in a surfing position down a snow-covered hill.  **R** _____

9.  Dimitrije Melovich based his snow-board design on surfboard _____.  **D** _____

10. The middle layer of clothing is worn for _____ against the cold weather.  **I** _____

11. In the giant slalom, the snowboarder passes through a _____ of gates.  **N** _____

12. One event for Olympic snowboarding is the _____ slalom.  **G** _____

Name: _____ Date: _____

# Level Three: Lesson 1: Famous Firsts

**Famous Firsts**

The wife of the President is called the First Lady. First Ladies influence the political and social life of the country. First Ladies represent their husbands at ceremonial events. These six First Ladies not only helped their husbands, but managed some "firsts" of their own. Read each description, and then guess which of the First Ladies is described.

> Abigail Adams (1744–1818)
> Lucy Hayes (1831–1889)
> Edith Roosevelt (1861–1948)
> Edith Wilson (1872–1961)
> Lou Henry Hoover (1875–1944)
> Eleanor Roosevelt (1882–1962)

This First Lady was the wife of the 28th President of the United States. When her husband got sick, she took over running the government. She decided who could (and couldn't) see the President. She decided which matters would (and would not) go to the President. This First Lady was the first to decode war messages and to issue orders to the military in the name of her husband. This First Lady was called the "Secret President."

**a. Who is she?**

_____

This First Lady was married to the 26th President. As a girl, she was quiet and shy. She loved books and reading. She loved surprises. One of her sons said, "When Mother was a little girl, she must have been a boy." This First Lady was the first to hire a social secretary. The secretary dealt with all the social invitations at the White House.

**b. Who is she?**

_____

Name: _____  Date: _____

# Level Three: Lesson 1: Famous Firsts (cont.)

This First Lady was the first president's wife to earn a college degree. She graduated from college when she was 18 years old. She was married to the 19th President of the United States. She became the first First Lady to travel across America. She was a popular hostess. She loved parties and enjoyed giving them. She was called "Lemonade Lucy" because she had alcohol banned in the White House.

### c. Who is she?

_____

This First Lady wanted to be called "Mrs. President." She spoke out strongly on political issues. She was the wife of the first Vice President of the United States. She was the first First Lady to live in the White House. Reading created a bond between her and her husband. This First Lady was the wife of one president and the mother of another.

### d. Who is she?

_____

This First Lady married her fifth cousin. She was the niece of another President. This First Lady urged her husband to support civil rights and the rights of workers. She was voted the most admired woman in America for 13 years in a row. This First Lady was the first to ever hold a press conference. She was also the first United States delegate to the United Nations. She was the first First Lady to appear in a movie.

### e. Who is she?

_____

This First Lady was the wife of the 31st President. She met her husband in a geology lab at Stanford University. She was the first woman to major in geology at Stanford. She and her husband often spoke in Chinese so those around them wouldn't know what they were saying. This First Lady was the first National President of the Girl Scouts. She was also the first First Lady to give a radio address. Her husband once described her as a "symbol of everything wholesome in American life."

### f. Who is she?

_____

Name: _____ Date: _____

# Level Three: Lesson 1: Famous Firsts (cont.)

## Reading Guide for "Famous Firsts"

### BEFORE READING

Before reading, "Famous Firsts," complete the **Before Reading** section of the Reading Guide.

### A. Prereading Activity

1. What is a First Lady?

   _____

   _____

2. In 2004, who was the First Lady?

   _____

3. Who was the First Lady before Laura Bush?

   _____

Name: _____ Date: _____

 # Level Three: Lesson 1: Famous Firsts (cont.)

## A. Famous First Ladies Word Search

See how many of these First Ladies you can find in the Word Search.

Abigail Adams      Edith Wilson       Lady Bird Johnson     Mary Todd Lincoln
Barbara Bush       Betty Ford         Eleanor Roosevelt     Lou Henry Hoover
Nancy Reagan       Hillary Clinton    Lucy Hayes            Edith Roosevelt
Pat Nixon          Jackie Kennedy     Mamie Eisenhower      Rosalynn Carter

```
O D B B H P Z B O U J G U T D K D N X F K N U W
R E V O O H Y R N E H U O L K K P P V U W C K M
T K W J C W A J T J C I W M A I T H O I C A D A
V N B G E D I T H R O O S E V E L T R Z N Q Q M
Q M K T R O S A L Y N N C A R T E R M A N B N I
Q Q O Z S Z Z T Z S O H E Z J W M U G X Z X L E
U N P S O J M H L S L D K J L B E A J Q K T O E
P A T N I X O N L E Z B E T Z G E Y F F I D C I
L T P J H O N I S V V U A E X R O G X B G Y N S
V U N U I L W F L M I E U R Y A I M Y Y D L I E
T E B Q J H P O A P A R S C B K C F F E K P L N
S L N H T H K H D D J D N O C A I A N L B S D H
I L Z I H L Y T Y F O A A R O Q R N C M C O D O
J W D G O U B A B U N J F L Y R E A E F E T O W
P E Q B S T B Y I T W K Q E I K R V B J J L T E
A S O A M J E T R X Q M V X E A O O L U S V Y R
J E N I Z O T C D P N T C I G O G Z N H S N R Z
U Y B F T M T U J I X E K A V B E I H A Q H A Q
S A O O K G Y Z O C I C N R G V B Y B R E I M W
Q H M Q J W F H H L A B B M Z K Z M Z A M L L F
V Y A O O I O X N J J O V B S F L U I P V X E H
K C J J H Y R O S E N O T N I L C Y R A L L I H
E U E H G B D C O C S D H M R Q X C Q D A U Q H
J L T O H U C P N O Z E R G R G A N J H F K Q X
```

63

Name: _____ Date: _____

 # Level Three: Lesson 1: Famous Firsts (cont.)

## B. Vocabulary for Famous First Ladies

| | |
|---|---|
| **press conference** | a question/answer session by the press with a public figure<br>*Example:* In the press conference, the press wanted to know if President Ford would pardon President Nixon. |
| **geology lab** | a science laboratory devoted to the study of earth science, especially rocks<br>*Example:* The scientists studied the moon rocks in their geology lab. |
| **National President** | the president of a nationwide organization<br>*Example:* She was the first National President of the Girl Scouts. |
| **radio address** | a speech given on the radio<br>*Example:* Mrs. Johnson outlined her beautification plans in her weekly radio address. |
| **political life** | the part of a person's life devoted to politics<br>*Example:* He dedicated his political life to promoting democracy. |
| **social life** | the part of a person's life devoted to interacting with other people in the community<br>*Example:* Because she was so shy, she had very little social life. |
| **popular hostess** | a giver of parties, teas, dinners, etc., whom everyone likes<br>*Example:* Everyone wanted to go to the Japanese dinner organized by this popular hostess. |
| **social secretary** | a person who deals with letters, notes, invitations, and social events for his/her employer<br>*Example:* Lucy was social secretary to Mrs. Nixon. |

Name: _____ Date: _____

 **Level Three: Lesson 1: Famous Firsts (cont.)**

## C. Prereading Questions

1. What do you think this reading is going to be about?

    _____

    _____

2. Read the questions in the **After Reading** section of this Reading Guide.

    a.  Which question do you find the most interesting?

        _____

        _____

    b.  Which answer do you think will be hardest to find?

        _____

        _____

3. What is your purpose for reading this story? Finish this sentence: I am reading to find out ...

    _____

    _____

## DURING READING

1. Put a check mark in the margin next to the information that answers the questions in the **After Reading** section.

2. Circle any words you don't know when you come to them in the passage.

3. Put a question mark in the margin for anything you don't understand.

4. Answer each "Who is she?" question as you read.

Name: _____ Date: _____

 **Level Three: Lesson 1: Famous Firsts (cont.)**

## AFTER READING

1.  READING THE LINES: Answer these questions by using information in the selection.

    a.  The wife of the President of the United States is called the

    _____

    b.  What are some of the duties of the First Lady?

    _____

    _____

    c.  Who was the "Secret President"? Why was she called that?

    _____

    d.  Which First Lady was the first to hire a social secretary?

    _____

    e.  Why was Mrs. Hayes called "Lemonade Lucy"?

    _____

    _____

2.  READING BETWEEN THE LINES: Answer these questions by inferring ideas in the selection.

    a.  Who was the 28th President of the United States?

    _____

    b.  Why do you think Mrs. Adams wanted to be called, "Mrs. President"?

    _____

    _____

Name: _____ Date: _____

# Level Three: Lesson 1: Famous Firsts (cont.)

c.   There have only been two women who were wives of one president and mothers of another president. Abigail Adams was the first; who is the second?

_____

3. READING BEYOND THE LINES: Answer these questions with your opinions.

a.   Why do you think Eleanor Roosevelt was voted the most admired woman in America for 13 years in a row?

_____

_____

_____

b.   Who, in your opinion, is the current "most admired woman in America"? Why?

_____

_____

## ASSESSMENT/REINFORCEMENT

**A.**   The National First Ladies' Library is located at 331 Market Avenue South in downtown Canton, Ohio. The library is a research and education center. Write for information or visit the library online at www.firstladies.org.

Name: _____ Date: _____

 **Level Three: Lesson 1: Famous Firsts (cont.)**

## B.  First Ladies Matching

**Directions:** Place the letter of the description on the right on the blank next to the correct term or person on the left.

_____ 1.  radio address

_____ 2.  Lucy Hayes

_____ 3.  social secretary

_____ 4.  Edith Wilson

_____ 5.  political life

_____ 6.  Lou Henry Hoover

_____ 7.  popular hostess

_____ 8.  Abigail Adams

_____ 9.  National President

_____ 10.  press conference

_____ 11.  Edith Roosevelt

_____ 12.  social life

_____ 13.  Eleanor Roosevelt

_____ 14.  geology lab

_____ 15.  United Nations

a.  The "Secret President"

b.  The part of one's life devoted to interacting with other people

c.  An earth science laboratory

d.  Someone who gives parties and is liked by everyone

e.  This First Lady could speak Chinese

f.  She was the first First Lady to hire a social secretary.

g.  A question/answer session with the press

h.  She was the first First Lady to earn a college degree.

i.  She was the first First Lady to live in the White House.

j.  The part of one's life devoted to politics

k.  Someone who deals with letters, invitations, and social events for his or her employer

l.  A speech given on the radio

m. The president of a nationwide organization

n.  She was voted the most admired woman in America for 13 years.

o.  An international organization devoted to finding peaceful solutions to the world's problems

Name: _____ Date: _____

# Level Three: Lesson 2: When Is a Planet Not a Planet?

### When Is a Planet Not a Planet?

Many astronomers believe that the planet Pluto may not really be a planet at all. The scientists who study stars, planets, comets, and galaxies think that Pluto may be an escaped part of Neptune. They think that it got knocked into its own orbit during the early days of our solar system. Other astronomers believe that Pluto formed from a ring of rocky, icy objects orbiting the sun.

Pluto is the smallest planet, five times smaller than Earth. It does not orbit the sun in the same way as Earth and the other planets. Pluto's orbit is elliptical. Its orbit is also tilted and crosses into the orbit of Neptune. Sometimes Pluto swings closer to the sun than Neptune.

Pluto has one moon called Charon that is almost as big as Pluto. Pluto and Charon are like twins orbiting around each other like a set of spinning dumbbells. They spin and move more slowly than Earth. A day on Pluto would equal a week on Earth. A year on Pluto equals almost 248 years on Earth.

Perhaps because of its size or its distance from Earth, scientists don't know very much about Pluto. Pluto is the only planet that has never been visited by a spacecraft from Earth. Maybe these are the reasons that the planet Pluto might not be a planet at all.

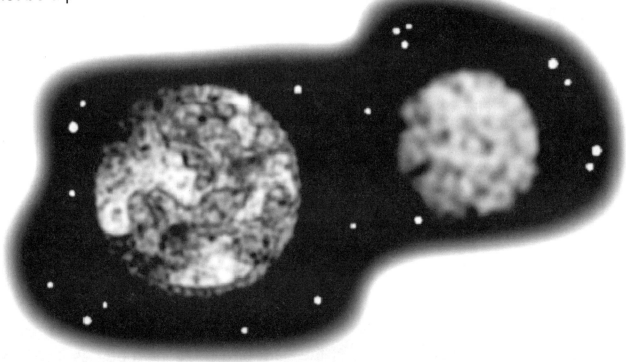

Name: _____ Date: _____

## Level Three: Lesson 2: When Is a Planet Not a Planet? (cont.)

### Reading Guide for "When Is a Planet Not a Planet?"

## BEFORE READING

Before reading, "When Is a Planet Not a Planet?", complete the **Before Reading** section of the Reading Guide.

### A. Pluto Facts

Research the following facts about the planet Pluto in an encyclopedia, textbook, reference book, or on the Internet. Two useful web addresses are:

        www.ajkids.com          www.enchantedlearning.com

1. The average distance from Pluto to the sun is _____.

2. The nearest distance from Pluto to Earth is _____.

3. The average temperature on Pluto is _____.

4. The diameter across the equator of Pluto is _____.

5. The number of known moons of Pluto is _____.

### B. Vocabulary

**Directions:** Match the vocabulary words in Column A with the correct definition in Column B.

| Column A | | Column B | |
|---|---|---|---|
| _____ | 1. planet | a. | a closed oval shape |
| _____ | 2. satellite | b. | an object that travels in orbit around a larger body |
| _____ | 3. orbit | c. | a heavenly body that revolves around a star |
| _____ | 4. elliptical | d. | the path of a heavenly body as it circles around another heavenly body |

Name: _____ Date: _____

## Level Three: Lesson 2: When Is a Planet Not a Planet? (cont.)

### C. Prereading Questions

1. Read the title of this selection. What do you think this story will be about?

   _____

2. Read over the questions in the **After Reading** section of your reading guide. Do you want to change your mind about your answer to question 1?

   _____

3. What is your purpose for reading this story? Finish this sentence: I am reading to find out ...

   _____

   _____

### DURING READING

1. Put a check mark in the margin next to the information that answers the questions in the **After Reading** section.

2. Circle any words you don't know when you come to them in the passage.

3. Put a question mark in the margin for anything you don't understand.

### AFTER READING

1. READING THE LINES. Answer these questions by using information in the passage.

   a. What are some of the reasons astronomers give for believing that Pluto may not be a planet?

      _____

      _____

   b. If Pluto is not a planet, what do the astronomers think it is?

      _____

      _____

Name: _____ Date: _____

## Level Three: Lesson 2: When Is a Planet Not a Planet? (cont.)

c. What is the name of Pluto's moon? _____

d. How long, in Earth time, is a day on Pluto? _____

e. How do Pluto and its moon orbit in space? _____

_____

2. READING BETWEEN THE LINES: Answer these questions that demonstrate your understanding of the facts and ideas in the passage.

a. What conclusion might be drawn from the reading about why Pluto might not be a planet?

_____

_____

b. In the first paragraph of the reading, what is another word for *astronomer* that is used by the author?

_____

_____

3. Which of these three statements about Pluto could you infer from reading the passage? Circle one.

a. Pluto is named after the Greek god who ruled the world of the dead.

b. Pluto must be very, very cold because it is so far from the sun.

c. Pluto is almost 40 times farther from the sun than Earth is.

4. READING BEYOND THE LINES: Answer these questions with your opinions.

a. In your opinion, should Pluto be considered a planet? Why or why not?

_____

_____

Name: _____     Date: _____

## Level Three: Lesson 2: When Is a Planet Not a Planet? (cont.)

b. Why do you think the scientists on Earth have not sent a space probe to Pluto?

_____

_____

## ASSESSMENT/REINFORCEMENT

**A. Directions:** Using what you know, what you have learned, and the Word Bank below, fill in the blank spaces in sentences 1–7 below. Some words will be used twice.

| WORD BANK | | | |
|---|---|---|---|
| Neptune | half | forty | moon |
| smallest | orbit | Charon | crosses |
| elliptical | 248 | farthest | ninth |
| spacecraft | star | Earth | 2,000 |
| 3 billion | tilted | elliptical | |

1. Pluto is the _____ and usually the _____ planet from the sun.

2. Pluto is the _____ planet in our solar system and the only planet that has not been visited by _____ from Earth.

3. From Pluto, the sun would look like a tiny _____ in the sky because it is almost _____ times farther from the sun than _____ is.

4. Pluto has one _____ named _____ that is more than _____ the size of Pluto itself.

5. It takes Pluto _____ Earth years to revolve around the sun once, and it has a(n) _____ orbit.

6. Pluto is about _____ miles in diameter and is about _____ miles from the sun and _____ miles from Earth.

Reading Engagement: Grade 3　　　　　　　Level Three: Lesson 2: When Is a Planet Not a Planet?

Name: _____ Date: _____

## Level Three: Lesson 2: When Is a Planet Not a Planet? (cont.)

7. Pluto does not _____ the sun in the same way as the other planets; Pluto's _____ orbit is _____ and _____ the orbit of the planet _____.

8. Some astronomers don't consider Pluto a planet because

   _____

   _____

   _____

   _____

**Bonus:** See if you can correctly label the planets on this diagram of our solar system.

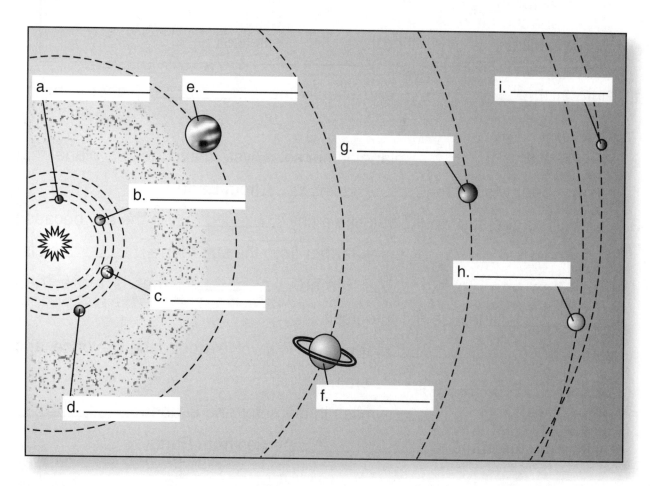

Name: _____    Date: _____

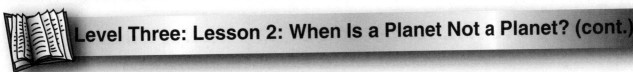

**Level Three: Lesson 2: When Is a Planet Not a Planet? (cont.)**

**B.  Directions:** Unscramble these words listed in the Word Bank that are asso-ciated with our solar system.

| WORD BANK |
| --- |
| sunspots      Earth         Saturn      nebula           Uranus |
| Mercury       atmosphere    Venus       solar eclipse    Mars |
| Neptune       Pluto         asteroid    galaxy           Jupiter |

1.  CMRERYU         _____
2.  DSAEOTRI        _____
3.  RTEHA           _____
4.  RMAS            _____
5.  BEULNA          _____
6.  ETUIJPR         _____
7.  SUEVN           _____
8.  LASOR CPLIEES   _____
9.  SSSOPNUT        _____
10. OPULT           _____
11. LAXYAG          _____
12. TNPNUEE         _____
13. UNASTR          _____
14. SARUNU          _____
15. SATOMRHEPE      _____

**C.  Directions:** Use the library, Internet, or other resources to list the nine plan-ets of our solar system in their order from the sun, starting at the planet clos-est to the sun.

1. _____    6. _____
2. _____    7. _____
3. _____    8. _____
4. _____    9. _____
5. _____

Name: _____ Date: _____

# Level Three: Lesson 3: Hey, There, Buckaroo!

### Hey, There, Buckaroo!

*"Mamas, don't let your babies grow up to be cowboys. They'll never stay home and they're always alone, even with someone they love."*

—E. P. Bruce

A cowboy's life required hard work, special skills, and lonesome hours. Cowboys, or buckaroos, as they were sometimes called, had to be strong, patient, honest, and trustworthy. Because the job was so difficult, only young people chose the life of a buckaroo.

People came from all over the country to be cowboys. Cowboys were Easterners, Midwesterners, Texans, ex-soldiers from the American Civil War, African-Americans, Native Americans, or Mexican-Americans. Some "cowboys" were actually "cowgirls."

Usually about 12–15 cowboys worked a ranch. It took that many cowboys to drive a herd of about 2,500 cattle to market. In the autumn, they rounded up all the cattle that belonged to their ranch and branded the calves not already branded. In the winter, they watched over the herd. In the spring, they chose the cattle ready for market. Then they drove the cattle to the nearest railroad town, which was sometimes thousands of miles away. At the railway station, the cattle were shipped to buyers in New York, Boston, or Philadelphia.

When cowboys were "on the trail," they slept on the ground in bedrolls. They were fed from a chuck wagon. They wore cowboy hats and cowboy boots. The hats kept the sun or rain out of their eyes. Hats were also used to carry water or to fan the fire. Cowboy boots were knee-high to keep pebbles, dirt, and water out. The spurs on the backs of their boots were used to encourage the cowboy's horse. Most cowboys wore a bandana around the neck. The bandana, or handkerchief, kept the sun off the cowboy's neck. If it was cold, the bandana could be used to cover the cowboy's ears. It could also be worn over the mouth and nose to keep the dust out. Most cowboys had a rifle. They used them to shoot coyotes and wolves that attacked the cattle along the trail.

Name: _____  Date: _____

At the end of a cattle drive, the cowboys were paid $50 for their work. The cook (who was also the doctor) was paid $25 for his services. After the cowboys got paid, they went to town seeking entertainment and new "duds." Entertainment was usually gambling and drinking in the local saloon. Shopping was for replacing cowboys' gear or clothes. The cowboy's gear, like bridle, saddle, lariat, spurs, etc., or clothes, like shirt, tight pants, hat, or boots, were chosen for their usefulness.

Often, competitions between cowboys sprang up. They competed for who was best at bareback riding, calf roping, steer wrestling, and bull riding. These contests led to modern-day rodeo competitions. Some cowboys still work on ranches. However, buckaroos today must be as friendly with their computers as they are with their horses.

Name: _____ Date: _____

# Level Three: Lesson 3: Hey, There, Buckaroo! (cont.)

### Reading Guide for "Hey, There, Buckaroo!"

Before reading, "Hey, There, Buckaroo!", complete the **Before Reading** section of the Reading Guide.

## BEFORE READING

Examine the drawing, and then answer the questions in section A.

## A.  Prereading Questions

1. What is a cowboy?

   _____

   _____

   _____

2. What does a cowboy do?

   _____

   _____

   _____

Name: _____ Date: _____

 **Level Three: Lesson 3: Hey, There, Buckaroo! (cont.)**

3. Where does a cowboy live?

_____

_____

_____

4. What does a cowboy wear?

_____

_____

_____

5. What skills must a cowboy have?

_____

_____

_____

**B.** In the list below, circle the names of those who were cowboys or cowgirls. If you don't know the person, research him or her on the Internet at one of the following websites:

www.americanwest.com/pages/cowboys.htm/
www.nationalgeographic.com/photography
www.ccsd.k12.wy.us/cowboys

| | | |
|---|---|---|
| Wyatt Earp | Annie Oakley | Davy Crockett |
| George Washington | Daniel Boone | John Wayne |
| Clint Eastwood | Willa Cather | Sam Houston |
| Jesse Chisholm | Calamity Jane | Roy Rogers |
| Will Rogers | Dale Evans | Buffalo Bill |

Name: _____  Date: _____

# Level Three: Lesson 3: Hey, There, Buckaroo! (cont.)

## C. Vocabulary

**Directions:** Use the words in the word bank to correctly complete the crossword puzzle on the next page. Not all of the "cowboy" words are needed to complete the puzzle.

---

### COWBOY WORD BANK

| | | | | |
|---|---|---|---|---|
| cowpoke | lariat | yucca | tenderfoot | chow |
| vaquero | spurs | stampede | poncho | adios |
| bandana | bunkhouse | herd | gringo | stirrup |
| bronco | frontier | denim | chuck wagon | horse |
| bandito | hombre | dude | chaps | |

---

## ACROSS

1. Newcomer to the West; inexperienced
5. Spanish for *bandit*
6. Used to rope cattle
9. A loop hanging from a saddle where the cowboy places his foot
10. Worn on cowboy boots to startle a horse to go forward
12. Spanish for *goodbye*
15. Lots of animals
16. A cowboy's most useful tool
18. Vehicle that carries cooking supplies (two words)
19. Food

## DOWN

2. Derogatory word for an Easterner
3. Remote area
4. Spanish for *cowboy*
5. A cowboy's neckerchief
7. Leather leggings
8. Mexican term for *foreigner*, especially an American or Englishman
11. The mass bolting of a herd
13. Dormitory for cowboys
14. Unbroken horse
17. Another name for *cowboy*

Name: _____ Date: _____

# Level Three: Lesson 3: Hey, There, Buckaroo! (cont.)

## Cowboy Crossword Puzzle

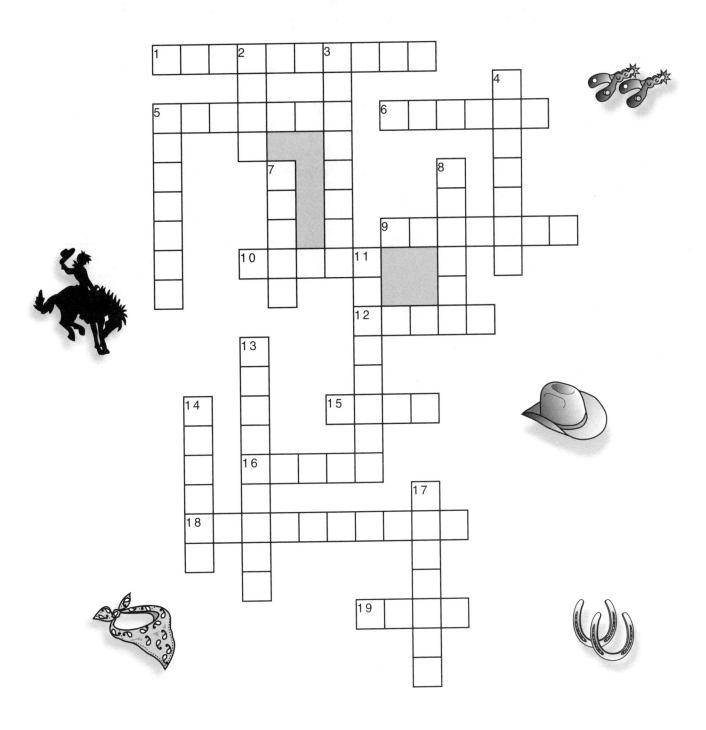

Name: _____ Date: _____

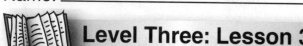

# Level Three: Lesson 3: Hey, There, Buckaroo! (cont.)

## D.  Prereading Questions

1. What do you think this reading is going to be about?

   _____

2. Read the questions in the **After Reading** section of this Reading Guide so you will recognize the answers when you read them.

3. It is always important to know what your purpose is in reading the text. Finish this sentence: I am reading to find out ...

   _____

   _____

## DURING READING

1. Put a check mark in the margin next to the information that answers the questions in the **After Reading** section.

2. Circle any words you don't know when you come to them in the passage.

3. Put a question mark in the margin for anything you don't understand.

## AFTER READING

1. READING THE LINES: Answer these questions by using information in the selection.

   a.  What do cowboys do?

   _____

   _____

   _____

**Level Three: Lesson 3: Hey, There, Buckaroo! (cont.)**

b. What do cowboys wear?

_____

_____

_____

c. Why does a cowboy wear a bandana around his neck?

_____

_____

_____

d. Describe the work of a cowboy.

_____

_____

_____

e. How much money did a cowboy earn?

_____

2. READING BETWEEN THE LINES: Answer these questions by inferring ideas in the selection.

a. Why shouldn't mamas "let their babies grow up to be cowboys"?

_____

_____

_____

b. What does the author mean by *drove* in the sentence, "They then *drove* the cattle to the nearest railroad town."

_____

_____

_____

# Level Three: Lesson 3: Hey, There, Buckaroo! (cont.)

c. What does, "... the nearest railroad town" mean? What is a railroad town?

_____

_____

_____

d. What is a cattle drive?

_____

_____

e. In the seventh sentence in paragraph 4, what does the author mean by "... to encourage his horse"?

_____

_____

3. READING BEYOND THE LINES: Answer these questions with your opinions.

a. Why was it important for a cowboy to have a good relationship with his horse?

_____

_____

_____

b. Explain some of the dangers and problems faced by a cowboy.

_____

_____

_____

Name: _____ Date: _____

## Level Three: Lesson 3: Hey, There, Buckaroo! (cont.)

c. How has the life and job of a modern cowboy changed from what it was in the past?

_____

_____

_____

d. Cowboys are known for their horseback-riding skills. Have you ever ridden a horse? Where and when? Did you enjoy it?

_____

_____

_____

e. Would you like to have been a cowboy in the American West? Why or why not?

_____

_____

_____

## ASSESSMENT/REINFORCEMENT

1. Explain what each of these idioms and expressions mean.

   a. to take the bull by the horns

   _____

   _____

   b. to flog a dead horse

   _____

   _____

Name: _____ Date: _____

## Level Three: Lesson 3: Hey, There, Buckaroo! (cont.)

c.  to get off your high horse

_____

_____

2.  Prepare a list of gear and equipment you would take as a cowboy or cowgirl going off on a cattle drive in the American West. Remember, this would all have to fit in a pack on your horse.

_____    _____

_____    _____

_____    _____

_____    _____

_____    _____

_____    _____

_____    _____

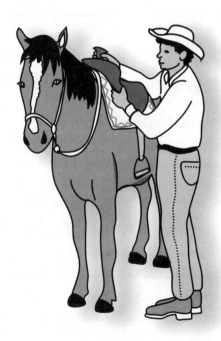

86

Name: _____ Date: _____

# Level Four: Lesson 1: Did You Know ...?

### Did You Know ...?

- Beavers like live, fresh trees rather than dead ones. Beavers work hard to fell and move parts of live trees. They like new trees because the limbs bend to fit the shape of their den. Dead wood breaks and falls apart. (Did you know that a beaver's den can last over 100 years?)

- Spiders are not insects. People often mistake spiders for insects. An insect has six legs. A spider has eight legs. An insect has three main body parts. A spider has two body parts. An insect has wings and antennae. A spider has neither wings nor antennae. (Did you know that spiders eat insects?)

- The language Ubykh became extinct when Tevfik Esenc died. The entire Ubykh population was forced to leave Russia and resettle in Turkey. Gradually, people who could speak Ubykh died, and their children couldn't speak the language of their parents. The last native speaker was an eighty-two-year-old man named Tevfik Esenc. When he died in 1992, he had this carved on his tombstone: "This is the grave of Tevfik Esenc. He was the last person able to speak the language they called Ubykh." (Did you know there are more than 300 different languages spoken in the United States?)

- The United States has more tornadoes than any other country in the world. About 800 tornadoes rip through the United States each year. Texas has about 140 tornadoes a year. As of 2003, Oklahoma City in Oklahoma had been hit by tornadoes 33 times in the past 90 years. The biggest tornado ever recorded was in Texas in 1971. This monster was over two miles wide at times. The busiest outbreak was the 24-hour period on April 3–4, 1974. One hundred forty-seven tornadoes touched down in thirteen states. The most destructive tornado known was in Shaturia, Bangladesh, on April 26, 1989. It killed about 1,300 people, with winds up to 280 mph. (Did you know that tornadoes can occur anywhere and at any time of the year?)

Name: _____ Date: _____

# Level Four: Lesson 1: Did You Know ...? (cont.)

- The Olympics are more than 2,500 years old. The first records we have are of the games held in 776 B.C. on the flat plain of Olympia. The Greeks held the games of Olympia every four years for more than 1,000 years. The games exemplified the Greeks' belief that body, mind, and spirit should be developed. The Romans banned the games in A.D. 394. Over fifteen hundred years later, the Olympic Games were revived. In 1896, the first of the modern Olympic Games was held in Athens, Greece. (Did you know that the five rings on the Olympic flag represent Africa, America, Europe, Asia, and Australia?)

- People around the world eat some pretty nasty things. Bats, scorpions, crickets, and tarantulas are just a few of the yummy treats people enjoy. The native people of Guam eat boiled bats, which they prefer with the wings and fur left on them. Scorpions are an Asian treat. In China, scorpions are soaked in wine and then deep-fried. In Mexico, you can buy a bagful of crunchy crickets to munch on. A Thailand delight is a big, hairy, poisonous spider. Tarantulas are served with coconut cream and lime leaves. (Did you know, on average, that an American eats 1,400 chickens, 21 cows, 14 sheep, and 12 pigs during his lifetime?)

Name: _____ Date: _____

# Level Four: Lesson 1: Did You Know ...? (cont.)

## Reading Guide for "Did You Know ...?"

## BEFORE READING

Before reading, "Did You Know ...?", complete the **Before Reading** section of the Reading Guide.

## A. Prereading Activity: Fabulous Facts

"Hey, did you know that ..."

- there are more horses in China than in any other country?
- a newborn panda is smaller than a mouse?
- hippos can run faster than humans?
- Smokey Bear has his own zip code: 20252?
- fish cough?
- an octopus will eat its own arm?
- mosquitoes prefer children to adults?
- snakes can't blink?

Do you know any fabulous facts? If so, write them here.

_____

_____

## B. Vocabulary

| WORD BANK | | | |
|---|---|---|---|
| poisonous | monster | language | fell |
| mistake | tarantula | modern | gradually |
| resettle | revive | cricket | destructive |
| antennae | exemplify | scorpion | extinct |
| population | Olympics | plain | develop |

Name: _____ Date: _____

# Level Four: Lesson 1: Did You Know ...? (cont.)

**Directions:** Match each vocabulary word from the Word Bank on the previous page with its correct meaning below. Write the word on the line next to the meaning.

1. _____ to cut down a tree

2. _____ to understand wrongly

3. _____ the long, slim organs of an insect

4. _____ no longer existing

5. _____ the whole number of people living in a country or region

6. _____ to establish a place in which to stay again

7. _____ changing by small amounts over time

8. _____ a means of communicating ideas

9. _____ a series of international athletic contests

10. _____ to show by example

11. _____ to bring to a more advanced or more perfect state

12. _____ to bring back to life

13. _____ causing ruin

14. _____ an arachnid with a poisonous stinger on its tail

15. _____ a small leaping insect

16. _____ a large, hairy, American spider with a sharp bite, not usually poisonous to humans

17. _____ containing poison

18. _____ description of the present time

19. _____ a strange and horrible creature

20. _____ a stretch of level ground that is treeless

Name: _____ Date: _____

# Level Four: Lesson 1: Did You Know ...? (cont.)

## C. Prereading Questions

1. What do you think this reading is going to be about?

   _____

   _____

2. Read the questions in the **After Reading** section of this Reading Guide.

   a. Which question do you find the most interesting?

   _____

   _____

   b. Which answer do you think will be hardest to find?

   _____

   _____

3. What is your purpose for reading this story? Finish this sentence: I am reading to find out ...

   _____

   _____

## DURING READING

1. Put a check mark in the margin next to the information that answers the questions in the **After Reading** section.

2. Circle any words you don't know when you come to them in the passage.

3. Put a question mark in the margin for anything you don't understand.

Name: _____  Date: _____

# Level Four: Lesson 1: Did You Know ...? (cont.)

## AFTER READING

1. READING THE LINES: Answer these questions by using information in the selection.

   a.  How long can a beaver den last?

   _____

   _____

   b.  How can you tell that a spider isn't an insect?

   _____

   _____

   _____

   c.  What is the name of the language that is extinct?

   _____

   d.  According to the reading selection, how big was the biggest tornado?

   _____

   e.  When did the modern Olympic Games begin?

   _____

Name: _____ Date: _____

 # Level Four: Lesson 1: Did You Know ...? (cont.)

2. READING BETWEEN THE LINES: Answer these questions by inferring ideas in the selection.

   a.  Why do you think Texas has so many tornadoes?

_____

_____

_____

   b.  Why did the language Ubykh become extinct?

_____

_____

_____

   c.  What does *native* mean in the phrase, "the last *native* speaker"?

_____

_____

_____

   d.  Why do you think the Romans banned the Olympic games?

_____

_____

_____

3. READING BEYOND THE LINES: Answer these questions with your opinions.

   a.  There are more than 300 different languages spoken in the United States. Can you name ten of them?

_____

_____

_____

## Level Four: Lesson 1: Did You Know ...? (cont.)

b.  What are some "pretty nasty" things Americans eat?

_____

_____

_____

### ASSESSMENT/REINFORCEMENT

1.  Have you ever seen a tornado? Have you ever been in one? Describe your experience on the lines below. If you haven't, write what you think it might be like.

_____

_____

_____

_____

_____

_____

_____

_____

_____

_____

2.  If you liked this reading, check out *The World Almanac for Kids* or *The Time Almanac for Kids*. They are full of interesting facts and figures.

Name: _____ Date: _____

# Level Four: Lesson 2: The Sun Queen

### The Sun Queen

Nefertiti was the most beautiful Egyptian queen in history. Her name means "the beautiful woman has come." She was famed throughout the ancient world for her outstanding beauty. But Nefertiti was unpopular with her people. She had many enemies. When this great Egyptian queen died some 3,300 years ago, much knowledge of her and the significant role she played in history was erased.

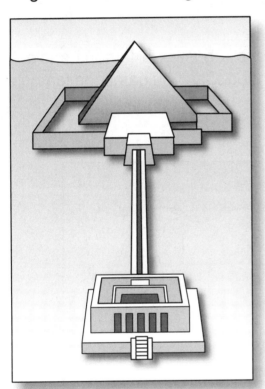

Nefertiti was the wife of Akhenaten. She and Akhenaten had six daughters, two of whom became queens of Egypt. She was stepmother to the pharaoh Tutankhamen. Some historians believe that prior to her marriage, Nefertiti was an Asian princess from Mitanni. Others think she was the daughter of a high official of one of the pharaohs. Most agree that Nefertiti was of royal blood.

Nefertiti was active in the religious and cultural changes initiated by her husband. They were monotheist—they worshipped only one god, Aten. Nefertiti was a priestess of the sun god Aten. The priests of the temples were threatened by this. They believed in many gods. They were polytheists. They didn't want to change. Nefertiti had many enemies.

When her husband Akhenaten died, Nefertiti became a pharaoh. For a short time, she was the sole ruler of Egypt. Because she had many enemies, it is not known how Nefertiti died. She may have been murdered. After her death, however it occurred, her name was chiseled off the monuments. On statues of Nefertiti, her face was defaced. The great city that she and her husband had built was razed to the ground; even the bricks vanished. They were stolen and carried away.

What Nefertiti is remembered for now is the painted limestone bust depicting her. It is one of the greatest works of art from ancient times. That exquisite bust of Nefertiti, housed in the Berlin Museum in Germany, gave rise to the tradition that she was one of the most beautiful women of antiquity.

Name: _____ Date: _____

# Level Four: Lesson 2: The Sun Queen (cont.)

## Reading Guide for "The Sun Queen"

### BEFORE READING

Before reading, "The Sun Queen," complete the **Before Reading** section of the Reading Guide.

### A.   Prereading Activity:  The Sun Queen

**Directions:** There are two drawings below. One is a bust of a famous ancient queen; the other is the country where this queen ruled. Can you name the famous queen and her country?

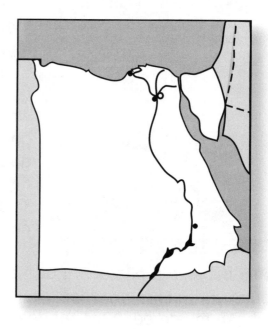

**A**                                             **B**

1.  The queen is _____.

2.  The country is _____.

           

Name: _____ Date: _____

 ## Level Four: Lesson 2: The Sun Queen (cont.)

**B. Vocabulary: Who? What? Where?**

**Directions:** Read the definition of each of these words, and then fill in the blank in each sentence (from the story) with the correct word.

**Nefertiti:** ancient queen of Egypt known for her amazing beauty

**Akhenaten:** husband of Nefertiti, Pharaoh of Egypt

**Egypt:** a country bordering on the Mediterranean and Red Seas

**Tutankhamen:** a Pharaoh of Egypt in 1361 B.C.

**Mitanni:** an ancient kingdom in northwest Mesopotamia

**Aten:** an ancient god of Egypt

1. They were monotheist, they worshipped only one god, _____.

2. Nefertiti was the wife of _____.

3. Some historians believe that prior to her marriage, Nefertiti was an Asian

   princess from _____.

4. For a short time, she was the sole ruler of _____.

5. _____ was the most beautiful Egyptian queen in history.

6. She was stepmother to the pharaoh _____.

Name: _____ Date: _____

# Level Four: Lesson 2: The Sun Queen (cont.)

## C.  Prereading Questions

1.  What do you think this reading is going to be about?

   _____

   _____

   _____

2.  Read the questions in the **After Reading** section of this Reading Guide.

   a.   Which question do you find the most interesting?

      _____

      _____

   b.   Which answer do you think will be hardest to find?

      _____

      _____

3.  What is your purpose for reading this story? Finish this sentence: I am reading to find out ...

   _____

   _____

## DURING READING

1.  Put a check mark in the margin next to the information that answers the questions in the **After Reading** section.

2.  Circle any words you don't know when you come to them in the passage.

3.  Put a question mark in the margin for anything you don't understand.

Name: _____ Date: _____

 # Level Four: Lesson 2: The Sun Queen (cont.)

## AFTER READING

1. **READING THE LINES:** Answer these questions by using information in the selection.

   a. Who was Nefertiti's stepson?

   _____

   b. What happened to the great city Nefertiti and her husband built?

   _____

   _____

   _____

   c. What does it mean to be "of royal blood"?

   _____

   _____

   _____

   d. Why didn't Nefertiti's people like her?

   _____

   _____

   _____

2. **READING BETWEEN THE LINES:** Answer these questions by inferring ideas in the selection.

   a. What is the main idea of this reading?

   _____

   _____

   _____

Name: _____ Date: _____

# Level Four: Lesson 2: The Sun Queen (cont.)

b.  Why did Nefertiti have so many enemies?

_____

_____

_____

c.  What does it mean to "deface" a statue or monument?

_____

_____

_____

d.  What is the difference between a monotheist and a polytheist?

_____

_____

_____

3.  READING BEYOND THE LINES: Answer these questions with your opinions.

a.  Looking at drawing A, do you think Nefertiti was beautiful? Why or why not?

_____

_____

_____

b.  In your opinion, should Nefertiti be remembered for her accomplishments or her beauty?

_____

_____

_____

c.  For which would you want to be remembered? Why?

_____

_____

_____

Name: _____ Date: _____

# Level Four: Lesson 2: The Sun Queen (cont.)

## ASSESSMENT/REINFORCEMENT

**A.** Research either of the following questions and write about it on your own paper.

1. How did the ancient Egyptians explain the creation of the world? Which gods played a role in forming the earth and bringing civilization to the people?

2. There are many mysteries that surround the life and death of Tutankhamen. What can you find out about him?

**B.** Write the correct word on each set of blanks below.

1. _ _ _ _ _ _ _ _ _ _ _  Those who worship only one god

2. Ⓞ _ _ _ _  Nefertiti was of royal ____.

3. Ⓞ _ _ _ _  Country where Nefertiti was queen

4. _ _ _ _ _ Ⓞ _ _ _  Nefertiti's husband

5. _ Ⓞ _  Aten was the Egyptian ____ god.

6. Ⓞ _ _ _ _ _ _ _ _ _ _ _  Pharoah who was Nefertiti's stepson

7. _ _ _ _ _ Ⓞ  Kingdom in Asia from which Nefertiti may have come

8. _ _ Ⓞ _ _ _ _ _ _  Egyptian queen famed for her beauty

9. _ Ⓞ _ _  This work of art gives us an idea of Nefertiti's beauty.

10. _ _ Ⓞ _ _ _ _ _ _ _ _  Those who believe in many gods

Use the circled letters above to complete the meaning of Nefertiti's name.

"the _ _ _ _ _ _ _ _ _ woman has come"

Name: _____ Date: _____

# Level Four: Lesson 3: Travel Guide

## Travel Guide

Most people use some sort of travel guide when they travel. Travel agents, travel maps, travel guidebooks, or travel tapes help modern travelers find their way. When Lewis and Clark began their expedition to find the Northwest Passage, they, too, used a travel guide.

This valuable travel guide was an American Indian woman named Sacagawea (Sah-cah-gah-we-ah). She was a skillful guide and a gifted interpreter. Sacagawea was strong, intelligent, and brave.

Sacagawea was the wife of a French-Canadian trapper, Toussaint Charbonneau, who had "won" her in a gambling contest from the Hidatsa Indians. As a young girl, Sacagawea, a Shoshone, was kidnapped by a war party of Hidatsa Indians. The Hidatsa were enemies of the Shoshone. They took her to a fur-trading fort in North Dakota. It was there that she became the "wife" of Toussaint Charbonneau.

Because they traveled through the land belonging to the Shoshone, Lewis and Clark needed a way to communicate with them. They hired Charbonneau and his wife, Sacagawea, as interpreters. Sacagawea spoke many Indian dialects and could also communicate through sign language. Whenever the expedition met with Indians, Sacagawea talked to them. She translated their words into Hidatsa for Charbonneau. Charbonneau translated the Hidatsa into French. A Frenchman in the group then translated the French into English for Lewis and Clark. This complicated arrangement was necessary because Lewis and Clark spoke only English.

Both Charbonneau and Sacagawea proved useful as guides and interpreters, and Sacagawea was especially helpful in identifying plants and searching for edible fruits and vegetables. When one of the boats tipped over, Sacagawea rescued the journals, medicines, and other valuables that were being swept downstream. Many other unexpected hardships were successfully overcome because of Sacagawea's quick thinking and courageous actions.

Sacagawea was a much-respected and admired travel guide. She was intelligent, brave, and resourceful. Lewis and Clark recognized the value of this special woman. Sacagawea's personal courage, sacrifices, and contributions helped make the Lewis and Clark Expedition a success.

Name: _____  Date: _____

# Level Four: Lesson 3: Travel Guide (cont.)

## Reading Guide for "Travel Guide"

## BEFORE READING

Before reading, "Travel Guide," complete the **Before Reading** section of the Reading Guide.

### A. Prereading Activity

1. Read the story and fill in the blanks from the words in the Word Bank. Not all words will be used.

| WORD BANK | | | | |
|---|---|---|---|---|
| a | buffalo | Indian | American | groups |
| at | clothing | Northern | States | one |
| Mountain | as | Utah | western | in |
| and | for | hunters | war | the |
| Shoshone | River | | | |

The Shoshone Indians are _____ group of North _____ Indian people. They lived in _____ Great Basin and Rocky _____ region of the United _____. The Shoshone belong to _____ of four regional _____ that are often referred to _____ the Plains Indians. The Western Shoshone lived in eastern Nevada. The _____ Shoshone lived in northwestern _____ and southern Idaho, the Wind _____ Shoshone lived in western Wyoming, _____ the Comanche lived in _____ Texas. The Shoshone were _____ and gatherers. They hunted _____ for food, shelter, and _____. The Shoshone were often at _____ with other Indian tribes.

Name: _____ Date: _____

# Level Four: Lesson 3: Travel Guide (cont.)

2. How many words were not used in the paragraph?

_____

3. What do you know now about the Shoshone people that you didn't know before reading this paragraph?

_____

_____

_____

4. What do you think the connection might be between this paragraph and the title of the Travel Guide story?

_____

_____

## B. Vocabulary

1. See if you can identify these things in the drawing below: travel agent, guide-book, travel map, travel videotapes, and travel guide.

Name: _____ Date: _____

# Level Four: Lesson 3: Travel Guide (cont.)

2. Read through this list of vocabulary words used in the reading to see if there are any you don't know or can't pronounce. Ask your neighbor, friend, or teacher how to pronounce the word or the meaning of the word.

| | | | |
|---|---|---|---|
| modern | valuable | trapper | kidnapped |
| travelers | interpreter | gambling | enemies |
| expedition | intelligent | Hidatsa | communicate |
| Northwest Passage | Shoshone | translated | complicated |
| French-Canadian | arrangement | cowardly | confronted |
| dialects | asset | explorers | edible |
| rescued | journals | medicines | unexpected |
| hardships | courageous | resourceful | contributions |

Pay attention to these words when you read "Travel Guide." If there are any other words in the story that you don't know, circle them with your pencil. Ask about them during the discussion that follows the story.

## C. Prereading Questions

1. What do you think this reading is going to be about?

_____

_____

_____

2. Read the questions in the **After Reading** section of this Reading Guide, so you will recognize the answers when you see them.

   a.  Which question do you find the most interesting?

   _____

   _____

Name: _____ Date: _____

# Level Four: Lesson 3: Travel Guide (cont.)

b.  Which answer do you think will be hardest to find?

_____

_____

_____

3.  What is your purpose for reading this story? Finish this sentence: I am reading to find out ...

_____

_____

## DURING READING

1.  Put a check mark in the margin next to the information that answers the questions in the **After Reading** section.

2.  Circle any words you don't know when you come to them in the passage.

3.  Put a question mark in the margin for anything you don't understand.

## AFTER READING

1.  READING THE LINES: Answer these questions by using information in the
selection.

a.  For what purpose was Sacagawea's husband, Charbonneau, hired?

_____

_____

b.  What languages did Charbonneau speak?

_____

_____

Name: _____ Date: _____

 # Level Four: Lesson 3: Travel Guide (cont.)

c. Identify the order in which these sentences *should* be.

_____ A Frenchman translated French into English.

_____ Charbonneau translated Hidatsa into French.

_____ Sacagawea translated Indian dialects into Hidatsa.

2. READING BETWEEN THE LINES: Answer these questions by inferring ideas in the selection.

a. Why did Lewis and Clark need an interpreter?

_____

_____

b. What were some of the things Sacagawea did on the expedition that made her so valuable to Lewis and Clark?

_____

_____

_____

c. The result was "She lived as a slave of the Hidatsa." What is the cause?

_____

_____

d. If the cause was gambling, what was the result?

_____

_____

3. READING BEYOND THE LINES: Answer these questions with your opinions.

a. In your opinion, who was the better travel guide for Lewis and Clark: Sacagawea or her husband, Charbonneau?

_____

Name: _____ Date: _____

# Level Four: Lesson 3: Travel Guide (cont.)

b.   What is the main idea of this reading? Can you say it in one sentence?

_____

_____

c.   **Research question:** In what year did Lewis and Clark hire Charbonneau and Sacagawea as interpreters?

_____

d.   What information in the Prereading Exercise, "The Shoshone," helped you to understand the reading better? Why was it helpful?

_____

_____

_____

e.   Why would it be important for Sacagawea to know sign language?

_____

_____

## ASSESSMENT/REINFORCEMENT

**A.**   Below is the American Manual Alphabet. Examine the sign for each letter carefully.

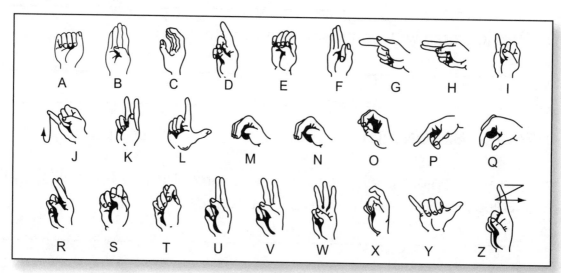

108

Name: _____ Date: _____

# Level Four: Lesson 3: Travel Guide (cont.)

1. Can you "sign" your name? Practice so you can do it without looking at the manual alphabet.

2. Write a very short message to sign to your friend. Then sign it for your friend and see if she or he understood.

3. Work on learning this sentence: "I am ( your name ); I come in peace." Why might this have been a good sentence for Sacagawea to sign on the expedition?

B. Draw a scene about Lewis and Clark, Sacagawea, or something else in the reading.

Name: _____ Date: _____

# Level Four: Lesson 3: Travel Guide (cont.)

**C. Crossword Puzzle:** Complete the crossword puzzle below using words from the vocabulary list on page 105.

**ACROSS**

2. Variations of a main language
7. Sacagawea's people
9. Enemies of the Shoshone who kidnapped Sacagawea
10. Someone who translates words from one language to another
12. Smart
14. _____ travelers use travel agents, maps, and guidebooks to find their way.
15. Toussaint Charbonneau was of French-_____ descent.

**DOWN**

1. Sacagawea proved to be an _____ to the explorers because of her resourcefulness and courage.
3. Describes something that can be eaten safely
4. Someone who hunts animals for their furs
5. Diaries kept by Lewis and Clark on their journey
6. Events and happenings that are difficult to deal with
8. The Lewis and Clark _____ needed a travel guide as they traveled west.
11. Lewis and Clark needed a way to _____ with the Indians they would meet.
13. Lewis and Clark were looking for the _____ Passage.

Name: _____ Date: _____

# Level Four: Lesson 4 : Money Matters

### Money Matters

> When does 2 plus 1 equal 4? When you add 2
> nickels and 1 dime, it is equal to 4 nickels!

Have you ever wondered who makes those nickels and dimes? It is the responsibility of the United States Mint to create, make, and distribute the coins we use as money. The Mint, created over 200 years ago, makes almost 28 billion coins a year. The offices of the U.S. Mint are located in Washington, D.C., but money is made in one of the four branches of the Mint: Philadelphia, Denver, San Francisco, and West Point.

The Lincoln Penny, the Jefferson nickel, the Roosevelt dime, the 50-state quarters, the Kennedy half-dollar, and the golden dollar are made either in Philadelphia or Denver. You can tell where a coin was minted by looking for the tiny "D" or "P" on the front of each coin (except the Lincoln Penny). Together, the Philadelphia and Denver Mints produce more than 50 million coins in 24 hours. These coins remain in circulation for about 30 years. In 2004, the U.S. Mint made two new nickels. Thomas Jefferson

**Left: Lincoln penny; Right: Back of a new Jefferson nickel**

will still be on the front of both nickels. However, the back will have either a picture commemorating the expedition of Lewis and Clark or a picture commemorating the "Louisiana Purchase."

The Mint also makes commemorative coins and medals. Commemorative coins from the U.S. Mint have been created solely for the purpose of honoring people, places, events, and institutions that have shaped our country. For example, there are commemorative coins for the Olympics, Sacagawea, and the anniversary of Orville and Wilbur Wright's Flight at Kitty Hawk, North Carolina. The Mint also makes medals like the Congressional Medal of Honor and the American Red Cross Medal.

We use coin money to buy things. Some of the coins, however, are beautiful pieces of art. The 50-State Quarters Program, for example, has beautiful artwork on the back of each state coin. The U.S. $20 gold coin shows Lady Liberty as a graceful, standing woman in a billowing robe.

Next time you have a coin in your hand, look at it carefully. See if you can tell where it was minted and when it was minted. And be on the lookout for those new nickels. Just think, you can have a little piece of history in your hand!

Name: _____ Date: _____

# Level Four: Lesson 4: Money Matters (cont.)

## Reading Guide for "Money Matters"

### BEFORE READING

Before reading, "Money Matters," complete the **Before Reading** section of the Reading Guide.

### A. Prereading Questions

1. What do you think the title of the reading means?

   _____

   _____

   _____

2. If you looked up the word *matter* in your dictionary, it would look something like the entry in Figure 1. Examine Figure 1 carefully.

---

**Main entry:** ¹matter
**Pronunciation:** ¹măt′ ər
**Function:** *noun*

1. a subject of interest or concern (a *matter* of dispute)  2. something to be dealt with: <u>affair</u> (personal *matters* to take care of)  3. a condition affecting a person or thing unfavorably (What's the *matter* with you?)  4. the substance of the universe: something that occupies space and has mass  5. material substance of a particular kind or function (vegetable *matter*)  6. <u>pus</u>  7. a more or less definite amount or quantity (cooks in a *matter* of minutes)  8. something written or printed

**Function:** *verb*

9. to be of importance: <u>signify</u>

---

**Figure 1**

Name: _____ Date: _____

# Level Four: Lesson 4: Money Matters (cont.)

3. According to this dictionary entry, the word *matter* can function as a _____

   or a _____.

4. Which definition of the word *matter* is the way matter is used in the title of the reading selection?

   _____

5. Complete the worksheet, "Coin Cents" on page 117 before going any further in the Reading Guide.

## B. Content Vocabulary

1. Complete the worksheet, "Dollars and Sense" on page 118. Then share and compare with someone else.

2. Use these vocabulary words in sentences on your own paper.

   branches          circulation          commemorate          expedition

## C. Purpose

1. Read the questions in the **After Reading** section of the Reading Guide so you'll recognize the answers when you read them.

2. What is your purpose for reading this story? Finish this sentence: I am reading to find out ...

   _____

   _____

## DURING READING

1. Put a check mark in the margin next to the information that answers the questions in the **After Reading** section.

2. Circle each vocabulary word when you come to it in the passage.

Name: _____ Date: _____

 # Level Four: Lesson 4: Money Matters (cont.)

3. Put a question mark in the margin for anything you don't understand.

**AFTER READING**

Answer these questions about money matters.

1. Circle the cities that have a branch of the U.S. Mint.

| | | | |
|---|---|---|---|
| Detroit | Baltimore | San Francisco | New York |
| Seattle | Kitty Hawk | Las Vegas | West Point |
| Denver | Philadelphia | Los Angeles | Dallas |

2. Which two branches of the U.S. Mint make the coins we use as money?

_____

_____

3. How many coins does the U.S. Mint make in a year?

_____

4. Draw a line from the coin to the corresponding president pictured on it.

half-dollar       Lincoln

dime               Jefferson

nickel            Kennedy

penny          Franklin Roosevelt

5. How can you tell where and when a coin was made?

_____

_____

Name: _____ Date: _____

# Level Four: Lesson 4: Money Matters (cont.)

6. Who is pictured on the $20 gold coin?

   _____

7. Explain what this last sentence in the reading means: "Just think, you can have a little piece of history in your hand!"

   _____

   _____

   _____

8. What is the main idea of this reading?

   _____

   _____

   _____

9. What does the word *commemorative* in the first sentence of the third paragraph mean?

   _____

   _____

10. If you could nominate a person, place, or event that shaped our country for a commemorative coin, who would you nominate?

    _____

11. Are there any parts of the reading that you marked with a question mark? What were they? Discuss with others.

12. How would you rate the reading material's difficulty?

    _____ too easy

    _____ just right

    _____ too hard

Name: _____  Date: _____

# Level Four: Lesson 4: Money Matters (cont.)

13.  How would you rate the reading material's interest?

_____  very interesting

_____  O.K.

_____  not very interesting

14.  How would you rate the amount you learned?

_____  learned a lot

_____  learned some

_____  learned very little

**Bonus:** What do you call a person who studies coins?

_____

## ASSESSMENT/REINFORCEMENT

### A.  Commemorative Coin

**Directions:** Design both the front and back of your own commemorative coin.

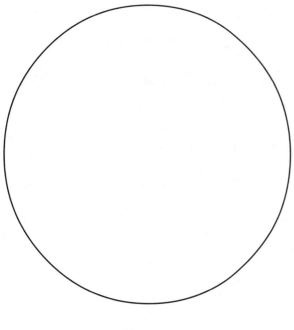

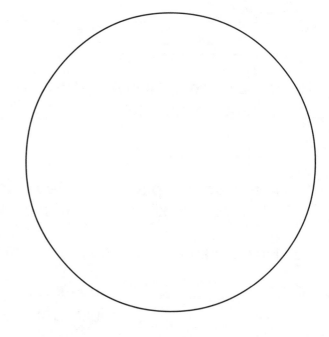

**Front**                                            **Back**

Name: _____ Date: _____

# Level Four: Lesson 4: Money Matters (cont.)

## "Money Matters" Coin Cents Worksheet

**Directions:** Read each sentence carefully. Choose the correct definition from the dictionary entry in Figure 1 on page 112 for how the word *matter* is used in the sentence. Put the number of the definition on the line in front of the sentence. The first one has been done for you.

____1____  a.  The tornado was the subject matter of the Special Report.

_____  b.  Does it matter if I am late?

_____  c.  What is the matter with you?

_____  d.  Mrs. Rodale refused to discuss the matter with him.

_____  e.  "This is no laughing matter!" Shelly cried.

_____  f.  The paragraph was about matter and energy.

_____  g.  Sometimes the brain is called "gray matter."

_____  h.  The stew was ready to eat in a matter of minutes.

_____  i.  Isaiah had to take care of some personal matters.

_____  j.  The patient's wound had filled with matter.

Name: _____ Date: _____

# Level Four: Lesson 4: Money Matters (cont.)

### "Money Matters" Dollars and Sense Worksheet

**Directions:** Match the people and events in the column on the right with the descriptions in the column on the left. The first one has been done for you.

__6__    a. The highest award given for outstanding courage in battle

_____    b. A guide and interpreter on the Lewis and Clark Expedition

_____    c. A gold medal presented to an organization for keeping people safe in emergencies

_____    d. Explorers who were seeking a water route across North America

_____    e. A series of quarters that celebrates the uniqueness of the states

_____    f. Aviation pioneers who created and flew the first successful airplane

_____    g. The place where the Wright Brothers flew their airplane

_____    h. The purchase by the United States of 820,000 square miles of North America

1. Lewis and Clark

2. Louisiana Purchase

3. Sacagawea

4. The Wright Brothers

5. Kitty Hawk, North Carolina

6. Congressional Medal of Honor

7. American Red Cross Medal

8. 50-State Quarters Program

# Answer Keys

## LEVEL ONE: LESSON 1: DANDY DAPPER DOGS (p. 6–14)
### BEFORE READING
**A.    Prereading Activity**

1–5   Answers will vary.

Paragraph: Check for three sentences.

### B.  Vocabulary
2.   The trainer works the dogs as the children watch.
3.   dog pulling a chariot, dog gettting the mail, dog rolling on a barrel, dog catching a Frisbee, dog answering the telephone, dog wearing a costume

### C. Prereading Questions
1.   Trick dogs

2a–b. Answers will vary.

3.   what tricks the dogs can do.

### AFTER READING
1a. Dogs did many tricks at a dog show.
  b. At a party
  c. Sybil: answered the telephone.
     Ramona: got the mail from the mailbox.
     Tamako: ran a flyball course
  d. They laughed, cheered, and clapped for the trick dogs.
  e. 4, 5, 1, 3, 2

2a. The children loved the dog show they saw at the party; any reasonable answer.
  b. Female, the pronoun *she*
  c. Sybil was the star of the show (oldest); Tamako was just learning (youngest).
  d. Good personality, lots of energy, smart

3a. Any reasonable answer
  b. Opinion with rationale
  c. Yes or no and why

## LEVEL ONE: LESSON 2: MANATEES AND DUGONGS (p. 15–21)
### BEFORE READING
**B.    Prereading Questions**
1.   Any answer that can be supported by the drawing.

2.   Any answer that can be supported by the drawing.
3.   In water, the sea, the ocean, rivers, canals, etc.
4.   Any answer is acceptable.

### C.    Vocabulary
1.   hot and humid     2.  hard or rough
3.   not deep          4.  warm-blooded
5.   died out          6.  man-made waste
7.   opponent          8.  person's or animal's actions
9.   pesters           10. animal nose

Sentence: Check for use of three vocabulary words.

### D.    Prereading Questions
1.   Sea animals
3.   what manatees and dugongs are.

### AFTER READING
1a. Manatees and dugongs
  b. Their tails–a manatee's tail is rounded; a dugong's tail is forked.
  c. 20 minutes
  d. back teeth for grinding plants, in paragraph 1

2a. Eating, holding things (like their babies)
  b. Hunted by man, driven away by pollution, people, noise, careless boat drivers
  c. Pollution, litter in water, crowded living conditions, lack of food (any three)

3a. "No Trespassing" signs, wildlife preserves, no littering signs, etc.
  b. Run over them, disturb the environment, throw litter into the water

### ASSESSMENT/REINFORCEMENT
A. a.  Both have the same body shape.
   b.  Both have the same tail shape.
   c.  Arms/flippers somewhat alike
   d.  Both can hold baby to nurse.

B. Accept opinions that are supported with reasons.

C.  1. mammals        2. tropical
    3. water          4. pounds
    5. teeth          6. gray
    7. flippers       8. swimming
    9. balance        10. extinct

** The only enemy of manatees and dugongs is: PEOPLE

## LEVEL ONE: LESSON 3: SLEEPWALKING (p. 22–29)
### BEFORE READING
**A.  Prereading Activity**
- A child sleepwalker opens the door of the house.
- The sleepwalker is about to trip over some toy on his way to the busy street.
- A non-sleepwalker saves the sleepwalker from a dangerous accident.

**B.  Vocabulary: Synonyms**
1. sickness
2. awkward
3. roam
4. growing up
5. bad dreams
6. kindly
7. hazardous
8. disasters
9. discard
10. fret

**C.  Prereading Questions**
1. sleepwalking
2a. Matter of opinion
b. Matter of opinion
3. about sleepwalking in children.

### AFTER READING
1a. 6–12        b.  Sleep
c. Walk around, repeat actions, wander
d. Don't try to wake up a sleepwalker by yelling, making loud noises, or shaking him.
e. Bewildered, confused
2a. May have had nightmares, in process of maturation, be stressed
b. general, widespread
c. No, because they will outgrow it.
3a. Opinion <u>and</u> rationale
b. It might startle or scare the sleepwalker.
c. Answers will vary.

### Sleepwalking: Crossword Puzzle

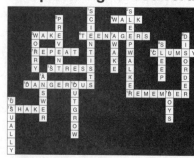

## LEVEL ONE: LESSON 4: THE CAT'S PAJAMAS (p. 30–37)
### BEFORE READING
A.  Check for three sentences.
### DURING READING
**A.  Vocabulary**
popular - A; territorial - A; aspirin - N; poisonous - A; reflect - V; vision - N; eyelashes - N; sunburned - A; frightened - A; excited - A; angry - A; breed - N; cuddled - V; carnivores - N; nocturnal - A

**B.  Reading**
1. Any answer, no matter how wild, is acceptable.
2. Cats
3. more information about cats.

### AFTER READING
1a. Max, Sassy, Sam, Simba, and Princess
b. To show that they like them
c. Look at its eyes
2a. Areas of land
b. It can make the cat sick.
c. Cuddle, talk to, hold the cat
d. Dogs are more social than cats; cats take care of themselves; dogs can do more tricks; any opinion is acceptable.
e. Any answer is acceptable.
3a. Keep it out of the sun.
b. Pretty good, but the relationship is more between cats and their homes.
c. Hold it, cuddle it, talk to it, keep it around people.
d. Yes, it is possible.

### ASSESSMENT/REINFORCEMENT
**A. True/False**
1. F        2. T        3. T        4. T
5. T        6. T        7. F        8. F
9. F        10. F

**B. Homophone Activity**
1. hear, very
2. not, in, sun, too
3. see
4. see, night
5. by, its
6. hours
7. to, be
8. not
9. know, there
10. four, their, paws
11. Some
12. no
13. meat, or
14. see, its, nose
15. to, your

## LEVEL TWO: LESSON 1: BRING IN THE CLOWNS (p. 38–45)
### BEFORE READING
**A.    Prereading Activity:** Accept all answers.
**B.    Vocabulary**
Column A: famous, coordinated, creative, comedian, confident
Column B: performing, acrobatics, juggling, balloon twisting, balancing
Column C: circus, rodeos, television, parties, movies
### C. Prereading Questions
1. Do; you; know; to
2. There; ways; to
3. to; one; ways
4. to; be
5. in; fairs
6. There; two
7. so
8. blew; to
9. I; it's; flower; eye
10. I; you; would; great
### D. Prereading Questions
1. Clowns, circus, or any reasonable answer
2a. Opinion
 b. Opinion
3. about clowns.
### AFTER READING
1a. A clown is a performer who makes people laugh and feel better about the world.
 b. Clown College, from another clown, experience
 c. Parties, circuses, television, on the street as a busker, fairs, rodeos, teachers, movies
 d. For juggling and balancing
 e. Bozo, Clarabell, Ronald McDonald
2a. The clown acts like he doesn't understand what's going on.
 b. Not everyone can make fun of himself or have the confidence and courage.
 c. A trick played on a person
 d. Distracts the bull's attention away from the cowboy
3a. Any reasonable answer

b. Any reasonable answer
c. Any reasonable answer
## ASSESSMENT/REINFORCEMENT
**A.    Drawings will vary.**

**D.    Word Search**

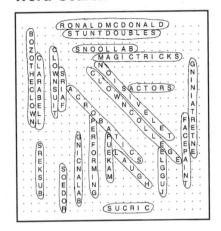

## LEVEL TWO: LESSON 2: THE JEWEL OF THE CARIBBEAN (p. 46–52)
### BEFORE READING
**A.    Prereading Activity**
Rain forest, flowering plants, waterfall, caves, mountains, coconut trees, beautiful fish, weather, beach, stingray, sunset, sea
**B.    Vocabulary** (More than one answer may be possible.)
1a. shallow          b. beautiful
 c. coconut          d. flowering
 e. lush             f. brilliant
 g. majestic         h. inviting
 i. perfect          j. white
2a. jewel            b. stingray
 c. surrounded       d. Jamaica
 e. Caribbean
### C. Prereading Questions
1. The island of Jamaica
2a. Any reasonable answer
 b. Any reasonable answer
3. the Caribbean or any reasonable answer
### AFTER READING
1a. Land of wood and water
 b. Caribbean Sea

121

c. White sand, clear water, beautiful fish
d. Flowering plants, hidden waterfalls and caves, insects, birds, etc.
e. It's so beautiful that for a minute the observer can't breathe.
2a. A sea creature with a flat body and a long tail
b. It is beautiful and valued like a jewel.
3a. Answer with rationale
b. Opinion and rationale
c. Opinion and rationale

## Word Scramble
1. coconut trees
2. plants
3. beaches
4. white sand
5. waterfalls
6. sunsets
7. rain forest
8. beautiful fish
9. sunny weather
10. blue water

## LEVEL TWO: LESSON 3: SNOWBOARDING (p. 53–59)
### Read/Stop
1. Tom Sims and/or Jake Carpenter, Dimitrije Melovich
2. Skiing, surfing, skateboarding
3. Snowboard
4. Answers will vary; rationale must be present.
5. 1998 Winter Games
6. Answers will vary.
7. Answers will vary. Be sure the rationale is there.
8. Set in motion; propel, push; shove, to drive forward; hurl; any of these
9. Boots, bindings, board, suitable clothing
10. Because it is a winter sport

### BEFORE READING
**A. Prereading Activity**
1a. A - skiing; B - snowboarding; C - surfing; D - skateboarding
b. All use boards; all do tricks with boards
c. Different boards; different weather; different surfaces (snow, cement, water)

**B. Vocabulary**
acrobatic, bindings, competition, experienced, giant slalom, halfpipe, launch, Olympics, resistance, surfing, technology, trench

**C. Prereading Questions**
1. Snowboarding
2a. Answers will vary.
b. Answers will vary.
3. what snowboarding is and how to do it.

### AFTER READING
1a. Opinion   b. Opinion   c. Opinion

## ASSESSMENT/REINFORCEMENT
### Snowboarding: Fill in the Blank Activity
1. Surfing
2. Necessary
3. Outer
4. Warmth
5. Bindings
6. Olympic
7. Acrobatic
8. Ridden
9. Designs
10. Insulation
11. Number
12. Giant

## LEVEL THREE: LESSON 1: FAMOUS FIRSTS (p. 60–68)
### Who Is She?
a. Edith Wilson
b. Edith Roosevelt
c. Lucy Hayes
d. Abigail Adams
e. Eleanor Roosevelt
f. Lou Henry Hoover

### BEFORE READING
**A. Prereading Activity**
1. The wife of the President of the United States
2. Laura Bush
3. Hillary Clinton

### Word Search

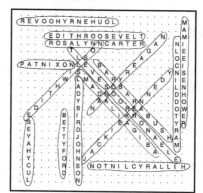

**C. Prereading Questions**
1. First Ladies; famous First Ladies
2a. Opinion
b. Opinion
3. Some First Ladies' firsts.

## AFTER READING

1a. First Lady

b. Support, stand-in for the President, represents her husband in ceremonial events

c. Edith Wilson, because she took over the running of the government after her husband's stroke

d. Edith Roosevelt

e. Because she wouldn't allow alcohol to be served in the White House

2a. Woodrow Wilson

b. Sounded more regal (opinion)

c. Barbara Bush

3a. She was intelligent, kind, energetic, cared about human rights and children's rights

b. Opinion

## ASSESSMENT/REINFORCEMENT

### B.   First Ladies Matching

| | | | |
|---|---|---|---|
| 1.  l | 2.  h | 3.  k | 4.  a |
| 5.  j | 6.  e | 7.  d | 8.  i |
| 9.  m | 10.  g | 11.  f | 12.  b |
| 13.  n | 14.  c | 15.  o | |

## LEVEL THREE: LESSON 2: WHEN IS A PLANET NOT A PLANET? (p. 69–75)
## BEFORE READING

### A.   Pluto Facts

1. 4.6 billion miles   2.  2.7 billion miles

3. -380° F      4.  1,430 miles

5. 1

### B. Vocabulary

1.  c      2.  b      3.  d

4.  a

### C.   Prereading Questions

1. Accept any reasonable answer.

2. Accept any reasonable answer.

3. about Pluto.

## AFTER READING

1a. Its tilted orbit; it swings closer to the sun than Neptune.

b. They think that Pluto was once part of Neptune or a ring of rocky, icy objects.

c. Charon

d. One week

e. Like a set of spinning dumbbells

2a. Because of its size and distance from Earth, we really don't know much about it.

b. Scientist

3. b

4a. Opinion and rationale

b. Opinion

## ASSESSMENT/REINFORCEMENT

### A.

1. ninth, farthest

2. smallest, spacecraft

3. star, forty, Earth

4. moon, Charon, half

5. 248, elliptical

6. 2,000; 3 billion; 3 billion

7. orbit, elliptical, tilted, crosses, Neptune

8. it looks and behaves differently from the other planets.

### Bonus: Name the Planets

a. Mercury      b. Venus

c. Earth      d. Mars

e. Jupiter      f. Saturn

g. Uranus      h. Neptune

i. Pluto

### B.   Unscramble

1. Mercury   2.  asteroid   3.  Earth

4. Mars   5.  nebula   6.  Jupiter

7. Venus   8.  solar eclipse   9.  sunspots

10. Pluto   11.  galaxy   12.  Neptune

13. Saturn   14.  Uranus

15. atmosphere

### C.   The planets listed in order:

1. Mercury   2.  Venus

3. Earth   4.  Mars

5. Jupiter   6.  Saturn

7. Uranus   8.  Neptune

9. Pluto

## LEVEL THREE: LESSON 3: HEY, THERE, BUCKAROO! (p. 76–86)
## BEFORE READING

### A.   Prereading Questions

1. A person who works with cattle or horses; accept any reasonable answer.

2. Takes care of cattle. Accept any reasonable answer.

3. Accept any reasonable answer.
4. Accept any reasonable answer.
5. Accept any reasonable answer.

**B.** Names of cowboys: Jesse Chisholm, Will Rogers, Annie Oakley, Calamity Jane, Dale Evans, Roy Rogers, Buffalo Bill (Distinguish between cowboys and actors playing cowboys.)

**C.** **Vocabulary: Crossword Puzzle**

**D.** **Questions**
1. Cowboys
3. about cowboys.

**AFTER READING**
1a. Ride, rope, brand cattle, drive cattle to market

b. Spurs, hats, bandanas, boots, shirts, pants

c. To keep the sun off his neck; to cover his ears; to keep dust out of his mouth

d. Autumn - round up cattle and brand them
Winter - watch over the cattle
Spring - drive cattle to market

e. $50 after a drive

2a. It is a hard, lonely life.

b. Herded them

c. A place where the train stops to load or unload passengers and cargo

d. Herding cattle from one place to another

e. By jabbing the horse with the sharp spurs, it startles the horse and makes it run.

3a. Because the horse was closer to the cowboy than anyone, and the horse was an

important tool

b. Stampedes - mass bolting of cattle outrunning the cowboy; sleeping outside on the ground; attacks by angry Indians

c. Cowboys now use trucks and computers more often to track movement of cattle.

d. Accept any reasonable answer.

e. Accept any reasonable answer.

**ASSESSMENT/REINFORCEMENT**
1a. Face up to the problem and get moving.

b. If the horse is dead, hitting it won't accomplish anything. Stop going over something that can't be changed.

c. You think you're better than the rest of us.

2. Accept any reasonable answers.

**LEVEL FOUR: LESSON 1: DID YOU KNOW ...?**
**(p. 87–94)**
**BEFORE READING**
**B.** **Vocabulary**
1. fell       2. mistake    3. antennae
4. extinct    5. population  6. resettle
7. gradually  8. language    9. Olympics
10. exemplify  11. develop   12. revive
13. destructive 14. scorpion 15. cricket
16. tarantula  17. poisonous 18. modern
19. monster    20. plain

**C.** **Prereading Questions**
1. A bunch of different things
2a. Opinion
b. Opinion
3. what I am supposed to know.

**AFTER READING**
1a. 100 years

b. An insect has six legs, three body parts, wings, and antennae. A spider has eight legs, two body parts, and no wings or antennae.

c. Ubykh

d. 2 miles wide

e. 1896

2a. Flat land, changing weather

b. Children wouldn't learn it from their parents.

c. The last person born to a place and culture

d. Because the Greeks favored them; they didn't want large groups of people to gather; or any reasonable answer

3a. Any 10 such as: English, Spanish, French, German, Dutch, Cambodian, Vietnamese, Farsi, Russian, Chinese, Japanese; answers will vary

b. Caviar - fish eggs; sushi - raw fish; anything similar

## LEVEL FOUR: LESSON 2: THE SUN QUEEN (p. 95–101)
### BEFORE READING
A. **Prereading Activity**
1. Nefertiti
2. Egypt

B. **Vocabulary**
1. Aten            2. Akhenaten
3. Mitanni         4. Egypt
5. Nefertiti       6. Tutankhamen

C. **Prereading Questions**
1. Egypt, Tutankhamen, Nefertiti
2a. Opinion
b. Opinion
3. who the Sun Queen was.

### AFTER READING
1a. Tutankhamen
b. People tore it down and stole everything.
c. Their ancestors are kings and queens.
d. She worshiped only one god; they thought she was too powerful; or any other reasonable answer.
2a. The Sun Queen was very beautiful.
b. Accept all reasonable answers.
c. To mess it up by drawing on it or breaking it
d. Mono - one; theist - believer; believes in one god
Poly - many; theist - believer; believes in many gods
3a. Accept all reasonable answers and rationale.
b. Accept any reasonable answer.
c. Opinion

## ASSESSMENT/REINFORCEMENT
B.
1. monotheists
2. blood
3. Egypt
4. Akhenaten
5. sun
6. Tutankhamen
7. Mitanni
8. Nefertiti
9. bust
10. polytheists
"the **beautiful** woman has come"

## LEVEL FOUR: LESSON 3: TRAVEL GUIDE (p. 102–110)
### BEFORE READING
A. **Prereading Activity**
1. The Shoshone Indians are **a** group of North **American** Indian people. They lived in **the** Great Basin and Rocky **Mountain** region of the United **States**. The Shoshone belong to **one** of four regional **groups** that are often referred to **as** the Plains Indians. The Western Shoshone lived in eastern Nevada. The **Northern** Shoshone lived in northwestern **Utah** and southern Idaho, the Wind **River** Shoshone lived in western Wyoming, **and** the Comanche lived in **western** Texas. The Shoshone were **hunters** and gatherers. They hunted **buffalo** for food, shelter, and **clothing**. The Shoshone were often at **war** with other Indian tribes.
2. 5
3. Answers will vary.
4. A Shoshone Indian is a travel guide for someone.

C. **Prereading Questions**
1. Indians, Shoshone, travel guides
2a. Answers will vary.
b. Answers will vary.
3. anything that has relevance to either the Shoshone or the travel guide

**AFTER READING**

1a. To act as an interpreter
 b. Hidatsa and French
 c. 3, 2, 1

2a. They only spoke English; they needed someone to help them communicate with the Indians.
 b. Sacagawea was a scout, interpreter, and guide; she saved supplies and valuable documents when the boat tipped over; she identified plants and edible foods.
 c. She had been kidnapped as a child.
 d. Sacagawea was "won" by Charbonneau.

3a. Sacagawea was the better guide because she could do so many other things that were helpful to the expedition.
 b. Sacagawea was a gifted and valued travel guide for the Lewis and Clark Expedition.
 c. April 1805
 d. Accept any thoughtful answer.
 e. In case she didn't know the language of those they met along the way

**ASSESSMENT/REINFORCEMENT**
**C.   Crossword Puzzle**

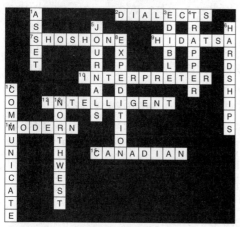

**LEVEL FOUR: LESSON 4: MONEY MATTERS (p. 111–118)**
**BEFORE READING**
**A.   Prereading Questions**

1. The reading is about why money is important, or it will be about money.
3. noun, verb
4. 1

**C.   Purpose**

2. why or how money matters.

**AFTER READING**

1. Philadelphia, West Point, San Francisco, Denver
2. Philadelphia, Denver
3. 28 billion
4. half dollar - Kennedy; dime - Franklin Roosevelt; nickel - Jefferson; penny - Lincoln
5. It is impressed on the front of the coin.
6. Lady Liberty
7. A coin tells where and when it was made; pictures on the coin tell the story of important people and/or events.
8. The coins we use for money are made at the U.S. Mint.
9. Memorial; in memory of
10. Accept all reasonable answers.
12–14. Answers will vary.

**Bonus:** Numismatist

**Coin Cents Worksheet**

| a. 1 | b. 9 | c. 3 | d. 2 | e. 1 |
|------|------|------|------|------|
| f. 4 | g. 5 | h. 7 | i. 2 | j. 6 |

**Dollars and Sense Worksheet**

| a. 6 | b. 3 | c. 7 | d. 1 | e. 8 |
|------|------|------|------|------|
| f. 4 | g. 5 | h. 2 |      |      |